Essays

David Rakoff

Essays

with illustrations by the author

Doubleday
NEW YORK LONDON TORONTO SYDNEY AUCKLAND

PUBLISHED BY DOUBLEDAY
a division of Random House, Inc.
1540 Broadway, New York, New York 10036

DOUBLEDAY and the portrayal of an anchor with a dolphin are
trademarks of Doubleday, a division of Random House, Inc.

Book design by Chip Kidd

Library of Congress Cataloging-in-Publication Data
Rakoff, David.
Fraud / David Rakoff.—1st ed.
p.   cm.
I. Title.
AC8 .R22 2001
081—dc21   00-052291

ISBN 0-385-50084-X

June 2001

The following pieces began their lives elsewhere in variously different forms: "In
New England Everyone Calls You Dave," "Arise Ye Wretched of the Earth,"
"Before & After Science," "Hidden People," "Christmas Freud," "We Call It
Australia," and "I Used to Bank Here, but That Was Long, Long Ago" on Public
Radio International's *This American Life*; "Including One Called Hell" and "The
Best Medicine" in *GQ*; "Extraordinary Alien" in *The New York Times Magazine*;
"Back to the Garden" in *Outside*; and "Tokyo Story" in *Condé Nast Traveler*.

FIRST EDITION

10 9 8 7 6 5 4 3 2 1

for

Simon Sutcliffe

and

Del Gordon

and

My Family

Contents

"You're maudlin and full of self-pity. You're magnificent."

—Addison De Witt

Essays

IN NEW ENGLAND
EVERYONE CALLS YOU DAVE

I do not go outdoors. Not more than I have to. As far as I'm concerned, the whole point of living in New York City is indoors. You want greenery? Order the spinach.

Paradoxically, I am about to climb a mountain on Christmas Day with a man named Larry Davis. Larry has climbed Mount Monadnock in southwestern New Hampshire every day for the last five-plus years. I will join him on ascent #2,065.

The trip up to New Hampshire will involve a tiny plane from Boston. I tear my medicine cabinet apart like Billie Holliday and still only uncover one Xanax. The hiking boots the outdoor adventure magazine sent me to buy—large, ungainly potatolike things that I have been trying to break in for the past four days—cut into my feet and draw blood as if they were lined with cheese graters. I have come to hate these Timberlands with a fervor I usually reserve for people. Just think, the shoes I wouldn't be caught dead in might actually turn out to be the shoes I am caught dead in.

I tell everyone about the trip, my voice singsongy with counterphobic false bravado: "*Guess* what idiotic thing I'm doing this Christmas!" I'm like Cloris Leachman in *Kiss Me Deadly,* trying to ward off her certain demise by telling the astonishingly talent-free Ralph Meeker to please, *please* remember her. Of course, things don't work out terribly well for her, and the very next time we see her she is being tortured to death.

It bears mentioning here that Monadnock is not Everest. It is three thousand feet high and the most climbed mountain in the world. It's not even a real mountain, so it would be freakish and abject in the extreme were I even to twist an ankle, to say nothing of actually dying on Monadnock. I would probably deserve it if either came to pass.

But I do not let this sway me from my worrying. I have other reasons for concern. For starters, I am only playing at reporter. I have never been sent anywhere on someone else's dime, relying up to this point upon my relentlessly jokey, glib, runny-mouthed logorrhea and the unwarranted good graces of magazine editors who just let me make stuff up. It takes all my strength not to call my editor and tell him that the jig is finally up, that I cannot do this piece. It seems too bad that the jig has to be up so far from my home in New York with its excitement, bright lights, and major teaching hospitals. The central drama of my life is about being a fraud, alas. That's a complete lie, really; the central drama of my life is actually about being lonely, and staying thin, but fraudulence gets a fair amount of play.

The connecting airline at the Boston airport has a fleet of maybe ten planes, all of them tiny, all of them serving rural New England. On the wall by the ticket window is a Season's

Greetings poster that is a collage of photos of the twenty-odd employees. They might as well be yearbook snapshots of the wrestling team of the high school I never went to. To a man and woman, they are healthy blondes in shorts and polo shirts, jostling playfully in the pictures, posed antically on a baggage carousel.

I sit, the only dark-haired person among the broad-faced butter eaters, wondering if my outdoors journalist drag—flannel shirt, jeans, most hated boots of Satan's workshop, down jacket—is fooling anyone. Across the aisle of the waiting area sits a fourteen-year-old girl, her face a somnolent mask of misery and hatred for the parents who sit nearby. Is my fakery as apparent as her anguish? She is outfitted in the teen Goth uniform: black jeans held together with safety pins, a torn black tank top, a black shirt over that. She has a tattoo of a small blue tear at the corner of her right eye—which should prove very helpful at job interviews in ten years' time. She could be a poster child for adolescent self-loathing, aside from the jarring fact that she is reading *Chicken Soup for the Teenage Soul.*

I break off half a Xanax and place it under my tongue, and magically, the brief flight to the town of Keene in an aluminum cigar tube of a plane is reduced to nothing more than a hazy, placid glide over snow-covered piney hills.

Although the Keene airport is not much bigger than a school cafeteria—and is of a similar, low-ceilinged, painted cinder-block style—there are no fewer than two signs that read "Attention! Any remarks regarding bombs, knives, firearms, and hijackings are taken seriously, as they are considered a federal offense." The slightest perusal of the airfield, essentially a large parking lot filled with tiny Cessnas and the like, makes it abundantly clear that poor Keene International (I guess flights from Canada are counted) must get a lot of precisely this kind of good-natured belittling humor; the aviation equivalent of shrieking in mock horror at a four-year-old in a monster mask who shows up at your door demanding candy.

I am disheartened to learn that the place where I will be staying is a bed-and-breakfast, not a hotel. My heart sinks. That means there is probably neither television nor phone in my room. And I have very little patience for what is generally labeled "charming." In particular Country Charm. I have an intense dislike of flowered wallpaper; ditto jam of all sorts. The former is in all-too-abundant evidence when I enter the inn, and the latter, I'm sure, lies in wait somewhere in the cheery kitchen. There is a knotty pine bar off the entrance hall with a settee with several embroidered pillows: "I'd rather be golfing." "On the eighth day, God created golf." "Golfers have sex in some humorous, golf-related manner," etc. On the windowsill above, a ginger cat is bothering a stained-glass butterfly ornament as the sunlight streams through the leaded panes. It is all I can do not to cry.

The proprietress is the kind of tall, stalwart woman of a certain age that used to be called "handsome." She is approximately nine feet tall. Her jaw is a feat of architecture, her eyes bright and resolute, her faithful dog Blue at her side. She smiles at me warmly and introduces herself as Hannah, extending a hand the size of a frying pan. "You must be Dave," she says. (In New England everyone calls you "Dave" regardless of however many times you might introduce yourself as David. I am reminded of those fanatically religious homophobes who stand on the steps of St. Patrick's Cathedral during Gay Pride, holding signs that say "Adam and Eve, not Adam and Steve!" I have always wanted to go up to them and say, "Well, of course not Adam and Steve. *Never* Adam and Steve. It's Adam and *Steven*.")

"You're in room three," she continues. "Why don't you go into the dining room and have some lunch and then we'll talk some. Come on, Old Blue Dog." In spite of myself, I am charmed. She puts on a dark green slicker and knee-high Wellingtons and is out the door, presumably to chop the ice off the pond, deliver a calf, or raise a barn.

I eat a club sandwich and drink some coffee to try to eradicate my Xanax buzz. I'm trying to appear legitimate, masculine, adult. Like I deserve to be there. Somehow it comes up that the waitress is going to Katmandu for the Peace Corps the following spring.

"Nepal. Golly," I hear myself say. (Who says "golly"? I think to myself. I'll tell you who. Katharine Hepburn in *The Philadelphia Story* and aging chorus boys in bellhop uniforms, walking through hotel lobbies with huge boxes of flowers.)

Larry Davis stops by the inn. I introduce myself and shake his hand in a hearty "hail fellow well met" manner. In return he gives me dispensation to climb the next day in my twenty-dollar plastic Payless shoes. I realize I have done almost no research for this trip, so I walk into downtown Jaffrey to check things out. This seems to me to smack of journalistic realness, a kind of topography-as-destiny-New-Journalism-Joan-Didion opening, perhaps. Perhaps I should do the WPA thing, go among the folks and observe their authentic and simple ways. Or maybe I'll try on a William Holden/Gregory Peck Paladin of the First Amendment type—all about the People's Right to Know—cracking open the festering lies of the town, controlled as it is by the despotic factory owner with the beautiful, virtuous daughter. "Things were fine in this town before that *writer* showed up!"

I am, as always, overwhelmed with movie fantasies. I think of that old standby, the star buildup where the camera wends its way through a crowded ballroom as the collectively murmured "Where is the Contessa?" plays on the lips of all assembled. Finally the camera stops on a woman, facing the other way, her creamy nape and lush hair. "Contessa," someone says. She turns around—it's Her!—her first close-up.

"Yes?" she answers, unmindful of her own compelling presence. Or the boy version, where our hero walks into town and the whispered buzz of intrigue thrills through the passersby. Lace curtains are discreetly pulled away from windows, and everyone wonders, "Who is the stranger?"

But it is Christmas Eve day as I walk into Jaffrey, and there is no one around to question my presence in their midst. I pass by All in Good Taste Gifts, Roy's Bike Shop, and the Jaffrey Bible House, which sells Christian gifts and, perplexingly, "supplies." The town is boarded up and deserted. I turn around and start to walk the two miles back to the inn.

Jaffrey is astonishingly pretty, particularly in the dusky Magic Hour of Christmas Eve. All clapboard houses nestled against snowy hillocks. I am taking notes by speaking into a little tape recorder. Perhaps that is what attracts attention. Or perhaps it is that there is not another living creature out at five P.M. on Christmas Eve, because a car passes and immediately circles back. The driver rolls down his window and asks me if I want a lift. I don't, but, How nice, I think. He drives on.

I am charmed by the congeniality of this interchange; how friendly, how uncreepy. I speak too soon. He circles back. He hands me a rectangular package in tartan wrapping paper. "Take this. It's the most watched video in the world," he says. (This man is giving me a copy of *Forrest Gump*?) "It's the life of Jesus." I beg off politely, claiming Hebraic immunity. He drives on. I make note of a copse of trees to my right. I will run and hide there until nightfall if he circles back a third time.

Here's an interrupting thought: If your therapist calls to reschedule your appointment—as mine just this moment did as I finished writing the above—and you make him laugh (as always), and if, in wrapping up, you say, "Well, I'll see you on Wednesday at twelve-thirty, then," and he responds, "I'm looking forward to it," is that bad?

I return to the inn, now wreathed in the kind of Christmas-in-New-England-Warm-Hearthed-Cheery verisimilitude that Ralph Lauren would burn down a synagogue to achieve. Nat King Cole's Christmas album plays at tooth-loosening decibels. I go upstairs and continue reading the new Truman Capote biography. I'm just at the point where Capote has started to dismantle his prodigious talent in favor of devoting his life to the two most completely nongenerative things in this world: gossip and the company of the too rich and too thin. Socialite Nan Kempner is quoted, apropos of God knows what: "I've painted my bathroom pink, because it helps in the morning not to have a white bathroom. Try painting your bathroom pink. It's amazing what it does to your skin tone. Don't do anything tomorrow that you can do today. Rush and get pink paint. It'll change your life." Oh, Nan, how true! I shan't put off things till tomorrow. I think wistfully of my own off-white bathroom far, far away, as my reflection gradually takes shape in the glass of the darkening windows of my phoneless, TV-less room.

The inn starts to fill up with families and couples who have come for Christmas Eve dinner. Alone and awash in unkind thoughts about Christmas and the countryside as I am, I stay out of sight for the most part. I can hear general revelry and prandial merriment coming from the dining room.

I go directly into the Bar of Golf Pillows. Hannah is there with a couple ("Merry Christmas, Dave"), as is a retired airline pilot who sits at the bar enjoying a decidedly un—New England cocktail with an orange slice, maraschino cherry, and pineapple spear crowding the glass. The bartender is a woman in a sweater knit with a portrait of a nuclear family of snowpeople. The wife of the couple also wears a sweater knit with a

smiling, holly-festooned teddy bear. The husband presents
Hannah with a very well rendered framed watercolor of a
largemouth bass. It's really good, and I say so. "Well, we'll put
it here to keep you company," says Hannah, propping up the
frame on the barstool next to mine. I make sure to look at it at-
tentively, my face frozen into the Art Appreciation rictus,
until Hannah and the couple go into the dining room.
Uncricking my neck, I order a steak and a red wine.

"Are you the Writer?" the bartender asks me.

The Writer. Finally. Despite the fact, or precisely because
this is just what I wanted, I reply, my voice far too bright, "Oh
God, no. I'm a complete idiot."

She doesn't entirely know how to take this. She gives me
the careful half smile one levels at a very large, possibly erratic
dog.

The pilot is the anti-me. A man so utterly comfortable with
himself that he can drink a cocktail with no fewer than three
different pieces of fruit in it and still seem the very picture of
adulthood. He talks a while about fixing up houses. It's what
he does in his retirement. Most pilots, he tells us, die within
two years of retirement, it's such a comedown after all that barreling through the ether at hundreds of miles an hour. His
voice is velvet soft and Atticus Finch authoritative, but there's
a sad whiff of mortality—a smell of old leaves underneath
everything he speaks of: the solitude of retirement, the no-
madic life of the career renovator, the trial and test of faith that
is building a butcher block island with sink, work area, and re-
cessed halogen light fixtures. It's a bit like watching *This Old
House* hosted by Baudelaire.

He leaves fairly early in the evening. I hope he has somewhere to go. Then again, I think, I don't have anywhere to go,
why am I so concerned with the imagined loneliness of a total
stranger? Then again *again,* I actually am somewhere. I am sitting in a bar of a New England inn on Christmas Eve. I am the

Writer, eating a steak, drinking alone, talking to the bartender. And even though I loathe animals, I lazily toss bits of
popcorn to Blue as he sits at the foot of my barstool.

It's just me and the bartender and my faithful dawg. Plus
my date the largemouth bass, whom I've been ignoring. I fairly
drip with authenticity now. I have let go of my paranoia. I feel
completely comfortable. So comfortable, in fact that, inexplicably, I find myself asking the bartender if there's either a synagogue or a gay bar in Jaffrey. I clearly feel the need to out
myself to her in every possible way. Why stop there, I wonder,
and not just go ahead and ask if there's a Canadian consulate
nearby?

She keeps refilling my wineglass as we talk. She cuts me an
enormous piece of baklava. More popcorn for the dog. I have a
mountain to climb in the morning, dammit.

My reverie is undone by the strange series of glottal kecks
and surds coming from below. I look down to Blue, whose neck
is arching forward and back in an ominously regular, reverse
peristaltic fashion. I find the words, as my voice Dopplers up
to a fairly effeminate and vaguely hysterical pitch: "I think
this dog might be getting sick. . . . This dog is getting sick.
The dogissick. . . . OHMIGODTHEDOGISSICK!!!"

Blue vomits out a small, viscous puddle for which, from my
quick and queasy perusal, I am largely responsible. The bartender cleans it up without a second glance. Thoroughly un-
masked, I settle up for dinner and take myself upstairs to
sleep. And to all a good night.

The logic underlying the truism that one should always travel
on a plane with a book is also precisely why bed-and-breakfast
culture is to be avoided if at all possible. Namely, you might
have to talk to someone. Talking to someone is not always a

bad thing—a great deal of viable human contact demands it—
but if, for example, one were getting ready to climb a mountain
of a drizzly, gray Christmas morning, with a fine mist of freezing rain falling, and no one has really either set up a breakfast
table or made it clear where the cups were stored, conversation might not be at the forefront of one's mind. Rather,
conversation that doesn't begin with the amusing gambit
"Where's the fucking coffee?" might not be at the forefront of
one's mind.

There are two women, mother and daughter, seated at the
only table that has any semblance of being set. There is also an
older fellow in a flannel shirt with suspenders. His hair is as
white as the china. If he is related to the mother and daughter,
it is not by blood. More likely he's a peripheral member of
their group, someone else's father-in-law, because his ceaseless joking would not be tolerated by someone who knew him
better. (And it is ceaseless. Moreover, it's the kind of joking
that stops all conversation stone cold dead: "Good morning."
"Now, are you sure about that? That it's a good morning?
Maybe it's only a fair morning." His eyes dancing with what
he clearly thinks is merry, elfin delight. After a slight pause,
and a small, diplomatic smile, the mother says, "Oh, now.
You're just a joker, aren't you?" like a weary waitress being relentlessly flirted with by a mildly annoying, but ultimately
paying, customer.)

The mother is in her mid- to late forties. It is evident even
now that she was once Beauty Pageant beautiful and is not unattractive now, but a mild Parkinsonian shuddering has rendered her tremulous and self-conscious. Her daughter is
twenty and, to give her her due, well spoken and quite cute—
her pores are tiny—but she is intoxicated by her own allure.
And, unlike her mother, she doesn't have the bone structure
to carry off that whole Mitford girl thing she has going on: all
high spirits, pluck, and verbiage. When she hears what I'm

about to do, she says, "Why, I was in a bar in St. Albans, Vermont, just the other night, and the subject of the Man Who Climbs the Mountain Every Day came up. All the way up in St. Albans. Imagine that." She says "bar in St. Albans, Vermont," as if she were saying "Les Deux Magots."

The floor of Larry Davis's car is deep with litter. Bottles, cans, wrappers. The kind of garbage accumulated by the very crazy. I am relieved to learn that it's detritus he's picked up meticulously from the trails of the mountain. When he gets a chance, he'll take it to the dump. Davis isn't all that strange a man, as it turns out, unfortunately for the magazine story, I think regretfully. Every smoking gun of possible derangement turns out to be as benign as the trash in the car. A man who tells you he is "a bit of an extremist" and, as proof, tells you of the day he and a friend tried every brand of beer they could find makes for somewhat monotonous copy, albeit decidedly better company, say, than the man who, making the same assertion, shows you multiple cigarette burns on his forearms and the human feces he has lovingly smeared into his hair and clothing.

I realize I have a child's concept of mountains. I assume they just rise up suddenly out of the flat ground, like breasts. (I also happen to have a child's concept of breasts.) It seems we drive for an eternity after we pass the sign at the entrance to Monadnock State Park, and I thrill briefly with the thought that we might just drive all the way, although I know for a fact that there is no road up the mountain.

We are climbing this Christmas Day with two of Larry's friends. It is three men and a baby. The climb begins easily enough, although I am somewhat alarmed to find myself sweating profusely after only fifteen minutes. I am hot and my clothes are starting to feel heavy and moist. Before we begin the earnest ascent of our trip, some 1,900 feet straight up within the next half mile, we stop at a spring to fill our canteens and take a short break. The water is fresh and exceedingly cold. I am asked no fewer than three times if I've ever had better water than this. I allow as probably not, certainly never colder water. Yes, that water is good. Very good. Boy, that is some good water, you betcha. But it is still, for want of a better term, water. Unless you spend your life drinking disease-ridden bilge directly from the Ganges or you live beside some strip mine's trace metals dumping site, extended discussions of water are a little bit like that annoying New York foodie habit of ascribing a "subtle, nutty flavor" to things with very little taste.

The guys are shooting the shit. "I gave Mona her Christmas present last night," one of them says, referring to a girlfriend. "My tongue still hurts."

A lot of the talk focuses on "1028s." ("Think we'll see any 1028s?" "That was a real good 1028 day." "All we need is some 1028s to make this a perfect Christmas.") Apparently, "1028" is code for babes.

I try to join in by asking them if they know the term 23 *skidoo*. They do not. "Well," I begin, "it's from the twenties in New York, and the Flatiron Building at 23rd Street creates this wind tunnel that, I guess, used to blow pretty young girls' skirts up, and the cops would signal one another that they could see the thighs of some lovely young thing by saying . . . uh . . . '23 skidoo' . . . it was part of the slang . . . you know, like, uhm, like 1028." *Flowers for you, Miss Garbo!*

Later, Larry asks us: "Hey, what's the difference between oral sex and anal sex? Oral sex'll make your whole day and anal sex'll make your whole week."

I am amazed. This is not really much of a joke at all, more of an observation, I think, and I find its relaxed, surprisingly positive attitude toward anal penetration a complete eye-opener.

"I don't get it," says one friend.

"It'll make your hole weak. Your H-O-L-E W-E-A-K. Get it?"

Oh. Good thing I didn't call forth a hearty "I'll say it will!"

The storm picks up rapidly as we ascend, rain and sleet falling and freezing immediately. The usual foursquare dimensions of evergreens, all staunch angles, needles, and propriety, are rendered Mae West voluptuous by a two-inch-thick coating of rime ice. Above the treeline, the last third of the climb, the temperature drops yet further by a good fifteen degrees, and the bare rock is glazed and dangerously slippery. My footing is becoming ever more precarious, and despite the crampons in our backpacks, Larry makes no motion toward stopping to put them on. He is testing my manhood, and also my temper. I say nothing and continue to climb. I am starting to get cranky. We finally make summit, its bare, wind-carved rock undulating: silver, pale, lunar, and glamorous. Shrouded in fog, we cannot see more than thirty feet in any direction. It lends a false sense of enclosure to everything, like a diorama from the Museum of Natural History.

And, no, I don't feel somehow better that we got to the top without the crampons, although I tell Larry otherwise as I take a long pull off a Sierra Nevada. I find nothing particularly ennobling about what we've just done. I'm not sporting any added tumescence; I have no sense that I've stared down anything significant. I find life itself provides ample and sufficient tests of my valor and mettle: illness; betrayal; fruitless searches for love; working for the abusive, the insane, and the despotic. All challenges easily as thrilling to me as scrambling over icy rock in a pair of barely adequate boots.

As a natural finale, the clouds begin to dissipate and a shaft of extraordinary late afternoon sunlight pours through and gilds a stretch of piney mountainside. Dusk is turning the rest of the sky into an indigo expanse pierced with hundreds of stars. The air is as clear and cold as vodka. Unexpectedly and with the speed and force of a freight train, I find myself quietly, desperately sad. I think, If I can only hear some traffic or if only the mist would part to reveal a parking lot—oh God, a beautiful, beautiful parking lot—down at the base of the mountain, I will get through this.

A hot shower and two drinks brightens my mood considerably. I am warm and feeling kinder, grooving, even, on my experience. I have invited Larry and a friend of his to supper at the inn. The Daughter from Breakfast comes up to our table. She asks about the day's climb. She is appropriately confident, clearly used to the attention of men. Larry and his friend are no exceptions; they smile and lean forward, laugh too loudly at what she says. She talks to Larry about his daily climb. "And how do you finance this *interesting* life with these daily climbs of yours?" she asks, her voice curling in on itself with playfulness. She is leaning on one arm on the back of my chair, her hips canted forward; her shirt rides up, showing a chevron of sleek tummy, a demure ring at the navel.

"I work," says Larry, suddenly cool. After a day spent talking about women—their absence on the mountain, their possible arrival on the mountain, the hypothetical projected excellence said arrival might embody—it is bracing and heartening to see that Larry knows when he's being high-hatted, no matter how unintentionally. Looking across the table at him, I see nothing but a surpassingly decent guy. Through the familiar blush of drink, I feel the familiar guilt of journalistic cannibalism, ashamed of my jaundiced scrutiny. He didn't begin his climbs five years previously in the hopes that a magazine writer might one day visit. By contrast, the mini test of my manhood notwithstanding, he was nothing but kind all day long. Everything about me, my inappropriate footwear, my effete lexicon, my unfamiliarity with such natural phenomena as trees, rock, and ice, have all been met with great equanimity and good grace. Larry and his pals are friendly. It becomes quite clear to me that the only one casting strange glances of disapproval my way is me.

At the summit I had pulled out the disposable camera I bought in the Boston airport. I made Larry take my picture a number of times. When the film comes back, I will look at the photos of myself, scanning them for evidence. Looking for the face of an adult. The face of a man who climbs mountains. The face of a Dave.

ARISE, YE WRETCHED
OF THE EARTH

Friday nights of childhood and early adolescence in Toronto were spent at the weekly gathering of the socialist youth movement of which my brother, sister, and I were members. Meetings were spent having earnest discussions of Marx and the great Labor Zionist thinkers like Theodor Herzl and A. D. Gordon; "bull sessions" about who in the group had hurt whose feelings; and air guitar contests to "Come Sail Away" by Styx. Occasionally the more dogmatic among us might even rise from one of the oily seat-sprung sofas and, with right index finger shaking and pointing heavenward, intone like Mayakovsky, "On Yom Kippur, we must go to a restaurant, sit in the front window, and eat pork!" A public *treyf* chow-down that would send an appropriate fuck you to the soporific comfort of our middle-class friends and families.

We never actually went through with anything remotely like this, of course, but in such teapot tempests are burgeoning political consciousnesses formed. We became deeply com-

mitted young socialists, ready at the age of fifteen for the ultimate prize the movement could bestow—a summer living and
working on a kibbutz, one of the collective farms that were a
central part of settling the Jewish state. We had been drilled in
all the facts: the kibbutz was the last bastion of left-wing Israeli
idealism; children lived in group houses away from their parents, a scenario of autonomous high jinks reminiscent of *Pippi
Longstocking;* kibbutz was the Great Experiment in Action.

Once there, we would meet other members of the movement from all over the world and spend many a happy hour en-
gaged in honest labor—laughingly baling sheaves of wheat,
picking olives, oranges, peaches, grapes, the sweat on our
brows a shining reminder of the nobility of collective farming.
In the evenings we would gather together and dance around
the fire while singing Crosby, Stills, Nash & Young songs and,
if one's older siblings were any indication, lose our virginity.
Years later we would renounce our bourgeois upbringings and
return to Israel, making lives of simple agrarian bliss.

The kibbutz I was assigned to was one of the oldest in
Israel, settled in 1928 by Jews from Russia, Poland, and
Germany. For the most part, our arrival was met with little to
no notice. We were just another group of volunteers, no different from the countless Europeans and Australians just passing through, taking time out to pick fruit, work on their tans,
and contract cystitis from their rampant and unchecked
coitus.

But we were different; we were members of the movement! I
thought that our political ardor would be immediately apparent. I had visions of our bus being greeted by garlanded folk-
dancing youth, so happy to have us there to share in their
lives. I had been raised on a fairly steady diet of just such socialist utopian Ziegfeld numbers: songs, film strips, and oral
histories that all attested to just this scenario. Trees weren't
simply trees, they were jungle gyms of plenty with smiling

children clambering over their branches; a field was somewhere you brought your guitar, so that your comrades could
dance down the rows after the day's work was over.

I was assigned to pick pears. Work would begin at four A.M.
and finish sometime midmorning, before the heat had set in.
How filled with fervor I was that first day, the light barely
dawning as I headed out in the back of the truck, wearing my
simple work shirt, a pair of shorts, and the traditional sunhat
worn by so many pioneers who had come before me to make
the desert bloom. (I should point out that we actually said
things like "Make the Desert Bloom" all the time. In fact, the
most mundane activities were habitually accorded classical,
romantic, politicized descriptions: "Breaking Bread with
Your Brothers and Sisters"; "Drinking Deeply of the Sweet
Water"; "Harvesting the Fruits of Your Labor," and so on.)

I know I sound like the Central Casting New Yorker I've
turned myself into with single-minded determination when I
say this, but the main problem with working in the fields is that
the sun is just always shining. Dyed-in-the-wool northerner
that I am, it became apparent after about two days that I was
completely unsuited to working outside, and I was moved
around among the kibbutz's various interior jobs: the furniture factory, the metal irrigation parts factory, and the
kitchen, assured all the while by the group leader that there
was nothing emasculating or jack socialist in being moved inside. After all, each according to his needs, each according to
his abilities. My abilities seemed to lie in passing out from heat
stroke after a scant two hours in an orchard.

This continued for weeks. It was a somewhat idyllic, if not a
mite monotonous, existence. Until the dreams of my socialist
future came to a crashing halt. Brought on, not surprisingly,
by an uncomfortable brush against the harsh realities of nature. The Long Night of the Chickens.

The boys of our group were gathered and told in the

hushed tones reserved for trying to avert impending disaster that we would forgo our regular work details and spend that night from midnight until dawn packing truckloads of poultry. Why this needed to be done with such urgent secrecy, under cover of night, and why the girls were excused was never explained to us. And we didn't ask. We greeted the news with that respectful Hemingway Silence of the Y Chromosome. No dopey girls allowed. It was all imbued with nocturnal, testicular melodrama, like some summer stock production of *Das Boot*. We slept that evening from nine to eleven—what I would come to know years later, in a far different context, as a Disco Nap. We rose and drank of some tea. The girls sprayed perfume into handkerchiefs for us to wear around our noses and mouths, and we were off in trucks to do battle with the insurgent chickens. The scene had everything but the diner waitress standing in the road watching us go, worriedly wiping her hands on her gingham apron.

The chicken coop of the kibbutz was a one-storied structure of corrugated iron, about half the size of a football field. It emitted a low rumbling, a vague buzz that you could hear from far away. And of course, from even farther away, there was the smell. A smell of such head-kicking intensity as to make a perfume-sprayed handkerchief almost adorable in its valiant naiveté; Wile E. Coyote warding off a falling boulder with his paper parasol. And the combination of floral scent and dung merely increased the vileness.

Chicken shit is horrible stuff. Unlike cow manure, which, according to David Foster Wallace, smells "warm and herbal and blameless," chicken shit is an olfactory insult: a snarling, saw-toothed, ammoniac, cheesy smell. Needlessly, gratuitously disgusting; a stench of such assaultive tenacity that it burns your eyes. Even the light inside the coop was smudged and grimy through the haze. Rather than making you never want to eat a chicken again, it simply makes you angry. It makes you hold a grudge. You'll eat chicken again, by God, and you'll chew really, really hard.

One of the barrel-chested Israelis shows us what to do: pick up four chickens in each hand. This is done by grabbing hold of the birds by one leg. "If the leg snaps," he says, "it doesn't matter, just to get four in each hand, *b'seder?*" he says. "Okay?"

He faces us holding the requisite eight, four in each hand, living masses of writhing feathers, looking like some German expressionist cheerleader, his pom-poms alive, convulsing, filthy. *Who will see their dreams fall away into the abyss and eventually succumb to the crushing sadness and meaninglessness of it all? We will! And what does that spell? Madness! Louder! I can't hear you!*

He crams the chickens roughly into a blue plastic crate smeared with wet guano. "And you close the lid, and *tchick tchack,*" he tells us, clapping his hands with "that's that" finality.

Before I even try, I know that I will not be able to do this. It is midnight, and we will be here until dawn or until the truck is piled to capacity with crated birds. I walk out into the sea of chickens. I reach down to grab one, its leg a slightly thicker, segmented chopstick. I recoil and stand up. I take a fetid breath, regroup, and bend down with new resolve, grab the chicken by its body with both hands, thinking somehow this might be preferable, although how I think I'm going to get eight of them this way, I'm not sure. Its ribs expand and contract under my fingers. A dirty, warm, live umbrella. I drop the bird as if it were boiling hot.

My friends are all grabbing handfuls of poultry and shoving them into crates, unmindful of splayed wings, attempted pecking of their forearms, and the horrible premorbid squawking of birds on their way to slaughter. My sensibilities are not offended by the processing of animals for food. I don't care about the chickens. I fairly define anthropocentric. I'm crazy about the food chain and love being at the top of it. But like the making of sausages, federal legislation, and the film work of Robin Williams, there are some things I would just rather not witness firsthand.

I leave the coop and go out to the trucks. Hoisting myself up on the flatbed, I start to help with the stacking of the full crates. I know that my unilateral decision to change my task is met with displeasure on the part of the men who run the coop, but I do not care. Their muttered comments are predicated on a direct poultry-penile relationship. I might as well have spurned the stag party whore, gone to the wood shop, and fashioned myself a sign that said "fag."

"*Ma ito?*" "What's the matter with him?" the head of the work detail asks when he sees me on the truck.

"*Ha g'veret lo ohevet ha tarnegolot.*" His friend has answered using the female pronoun when referring to me. "The lady doesn't like the chickens."

It would be years before I was referred to as "she" again. And then very rarely and only as a joke by friends. Calling each other "she" is not quite the mainstay of the lexicon of the urban homosexual as people think. It is not our "Make the Desert Bloom."

I turn around to look at the men, making it quite clear to them that I understand what they are saying. The man who called me "she" avoids my eyes and busies himself with straightening a pile of crates and tightening the tarpaulin on the side of the truck.

"You're right," I tell him in Hebrew. "*She* doesn't like the chickens."

Have you ever had one of those moments when you know that you are being visited by your own future? They come so rarely and with so little fanfare, those moments. They are not particularly photogenic, there is no breach in the clouds to reveal the shining city on a hill, no folk-dancing children outside your bus, no production values to speak of. Just a glimpse of such quotidian, incontrovertible truth that, after the initial shock at the supreme weirdness of it all, a kind of calm sets in. So this is to be my life.

At that very moment I saw that I would never live on a kibbutz. I would not lose my virginity that summer to any of the girls from the group. Indeed, I would not care to do so. I am grateful to that macho blowhard. He made me consciously realize what I had always known but been somehow unable to say to myself: He's right, I don't like chickens . . . I like men.

Now I live in the city that might best be described as the un-kibbutz. Where nobody would dream of touching a live chicken. Where whatever spirit of collectivist altruism people might have had dried up long ago, and where the words *Karl* and *Marx* generally bring up associations of Lagerfeld and Groucho.

At socialist summer camp in northern Ontario, I and the other children of affluent professionals would gather under the trees every day to sing before going in to lunch. One of the songs was always "The Internationale," that worldwide hymn of the proletariat. One summer we were even taught to sing it with our left fists raised. We were, none of us, by any stretch of the imagination what could be described as prisoners of starvation or enthralled slaves, admittedly, both catchier metaphors and easier to scan than "Arise, ye children of psychiatrists." But they had little to nothing to do with us personally. Yet for those few moments when we were singing, those words seemed so true. How can I describe to you that eleven-year-old's sense of purpose? Like the patrons of Rick's bar in *Casablanca* who manage to drown out the Germans with the "Marseillaise," I was overcome by the thrill of belonging to some larger purpose, something outside of my own body. The sheer heart-stopping beauty of a world of justice and perfection, rising on new foundations. And that one line, "We have been naught. We shall be all." Naught. What a wonderful word to describe my insignificance. It spoke as much about my wish to be delivered from this preadolescent self as it did to any consciousness of liberating the masses, but it held such promise of what I might hope for that even now, as I write this, I can still call up that old fervor. It still makes my breath catch in my throat.

LUSH LIFE

We were a quorum of spores, a federation of fleas. Present yet wholly insignificant. Collectively mobilized, we might at best have hoped to rise up as an unsightly mold or a bothersome itch. Mostly, though, we got drunk. This, we decided, was how we would survive our jobs as assistants in publishing.

Youth is not wasted on the young, it is perpetrated on the young.

With disturbing regularity, the end of the work day found us at the old Monkey Bar, the Dorset Bar, the Warwick Bar, all attached to serviceable and somewhat down-at-heel hotels. Midtown Manhattan used to be full of just such comfortably shabby establishments where career waiters with brilliantined comb-overs and shiny-elbowed jackets might serve marvelously cheap albeit watery drinks, along with free snacks: withered celery sticks; pretzel nuggets accompanying a cheese spread of a color that in nature usually signals "I am an alluring yet highly poisonous tree frog, beware!"; chicken wings kept barely, salmonella-friendly warm in a chafing dish over a Sterno lamp; and a bounty of unironic, faux Asian, pupu platter dough cylinders, pockets, and triangles that were—oh glory!—fried. Dinner and forgetfulness all for ten dollars. We were also provided a welcome degree of anonymity. In unhappening bars like these, we would never have to run into our classmates from college whose twenties were not turning out to be wretched, who were now making upward of six figures in their law and finance jobs. Those with expense accounts tended not to frequent a place, as we did, simply because they had heard that the management didn't stint on the miniature pigs in blankets.

We were not mining coal. We were not even waiting tables. We worked in books, and we did so willingly. Complicit believers in the mythic glamour of a literary New York and our eventual and rightful places therein. Yet still we gathered like wounded veterans of some great war, crystallizing around our despair, our outrage fueled by our outsize sense of entitlement. In truth, in the only work that paid less than being an editorial assistant, you at least got to eat as much chicken as you wanted once the oil had been turned off for the night.

Hooch, happily, was still one luxury we could afford. Our drunkenness was twofold: there was the liquor, and there was also the intoxication brought on by the self-aggrandizing conviction that we happy few, we Cheery Boozehounds, were the new incarnations of that most mythic bunch of souses: the Algonquin Round Table. This pipe dream sustained not just us, but I suspect countless other tables of publishing menials all over town. So desperate were we to assume the mantles of Parker, Benchley, and their ilk that we weren't going to let some silly thing like a dearth of wit or the complete absence of a body of work on any of our parts deter us. With enough four-dollar drinks sloshing through our veins, even the most dunderheaded, schoolyard japery qualified as coruscating repartee. "What do you want? A medal or a chest to pin it on?" would elicit merry cries of "Oh, touché!" as we clutched our martinis, throwing our heads back in mirthless, weary laughter.

That represented the high point of the discourse, before our tongues thickened and our moods darkened unpleasantly. As the evenings wore on, a hostile, gin-scented pall fell over everything, and our glittering aphorisms were reduced to the wishful and direct "I hope my boss is dead right now." Paying the bill, we stumbled out into the street and back to our apartments, where we spent the rest of the night jealously reading the manuscripts of those who actually wrote and didn't just drink about it. Rising, unrefreshed, we would return to the office and, rubbing alcohol and cotton balls in hand, get down to work swabbing, leaf by leaf, the potted plants in our bosses' offices, a vain attempt to stop the outbreak of white fly that was going around the floor.

At least, we consoled ourselves, we were assistants, not secretaries. It's a loathsome distinction, the almost meaningless difference between field and house slave. We all of us, secretaries and assistants alike, had much the same duties—filing, photocopying, taking dictation, and making reservations for meals we would never get to eat—although the secretaries made significantly more money than we did. What we could not see in our fugue state of self-pity at that time is that there was an all-too-real distinction. Unlike the secretaries, whose salaries dwarfed ours in the moment but would probably stay where they were for years to come, our penury came with the promise that we were bound for better things; we would be mentored, promoted, and one day raised to our rightful stations as book editors, our faith in the East Coast meritocracy restored.

Still, every April, when National Secretary's Day rolled around, many of us took sick days, genuinely nauseous with worry that we be mistook and there, on our *assistants'* desks, would be the asparagus-fern-and-baby's-breath-surrounded long-stemmed roses with the card from the boss who "just couldn't do it withoutcha!" It would be too raw a truth telling, like getting a "Happy Anniversary of Our Loveless Marriage" card.

There would be only one way out, and that was up. But, we were told, dues would have to be paid. It would take a very long time, and it would happen only to the very best among us. (This was before many of us realized that there was, of course, another way out. Out.)

We spent an inordinate amount of time minutely parsing our own movements. I don't recall us being competitive with one another so much as practicing a kind of Kremlinology, attaching disproportionate significance to our message-taking skills, complimenting one another on our collating acumen— no small feat from under a hovering cloud of job hatred—and hoping against hope that our bosses had noticed the crispness of our penmanship, the ease with which the table at Michael's had been procured, and the precision of the right angles of the papers on our desks; aerial photographs of patchwork farms of Post-it yellow and While You Were Out pink.

Impressing the higher-ups became our constant purpose. How sad to realize from the vantage point of years later that, like the poor gnat on the bull's horn, the answer to that perpetual question, "What do they think of me?" was: they didn't. At all. At best we might hope for the sporadically noticed but generally benignly ignored presence of Asta, the dog from the *Thin Man* movies. And there were times when it all seemed like a fantastic whirl of Nick and Nora Charles, with us sitting in the backseat, tongues lolling out, blissfully purling drops of saliva into the passing breeze, just so happy to be along for the ride. ("Yes, sir, Mr. Rushdie, right away.") But there was always that danger in feeling like pals—or, more perilously, colleagues—with one's boss, a delusion that by definition will bite you in the ass. No one ever shot the scene of what it was like to be Asta on the cold, bright, hung-over morning after an evening of badinage and hours of genteel tippling. A morning where Myrna Loy, her hair matted and a taste for blood in her rank mouth, baits and emasculates William Powell until he lashes out and finds the closest and easiest thing to kick, which is guess who? We were the help, and it was best not to forget it.

Seemingly daily, the bosses safely at lunch, I would stand at the entrance of Sheila's cubicle, as if at a lectern: "Well, Bob came home last night." I would begin in a small voice and then sigh, the weight of the world almost too heavy on my shoulders, the breath breaking up into a voice cracked with incipient tears. "And he cried like a baby in my arms. And he said he was so sorry and that it was me and the kids all the way."

By this point my face would be crumpled in weeping while Sheila's crumpled in joy, as she laughingly lit up another cigarette, eagerly awaiting the punch line she knew by heart, reciting it along with me: "And he said that when my jaw healed, we could take that trip to Colorado like he promised."

Sheila was our bad girl leader. A poet and writer herself, she despised her job and didn't care who knew it, smoking openly at her desk and standing on ceremony for no one. "These would be my pajamas that I slept in last night," she would say, indicating the black long-sleeved T-shirt and black workout pants she was wearing. "And *this*," she would add, fingering a crusted white smear on the hem of the top, "this would be spilled food. Nice. Well, they say 'dress for the job you want, not the job you have.' "

It was immediately to Sheila that I went when I received my birthday card. It was late November, months past *that* day in April; I suppose my guard was down. I had also by this time started taking baby steps on the path toward liberation. I was now an assistant editor, a promotion that came with an infinitesimal increase in salary and an even tinier change in my actual duties. I was given an excessively generous gift from the exacting boss whom, in spite of everything, I adored and who adored me right back (woof woof!). Opening the envelope, my eyes fell upon the card. It was one of those tinted B-movie stills from the 1950s. A woman in a smart worsted business jacket, wearing a pair of glasses at which men seldom make passes, and a switchboard operator's headset, out of which were shooting tiny lightning bolts, was shown to be thinking, Someone needs coffee! Above her head, in screaming sci-fi acid-yellow type, was the title of this card's purported movie: *The Amazing Tale of the Psychic Secretary.*

A woman with a disfiguringly hunched back yearns for love and finally finds it with a handsome young man who adores her.

    "But what about my back?" she asks. "Surely that must repulse you."

    "Nonsense," said the man.

    "The fact that I might never properly look you in the face, doesn't that make you hate me just a little bit?"

    "Not at all!" the man cried. "I think you're beautiful just the way you are and I love you and I want you to meet my parents!"

    So, one fine Sunday in spring, they drive down to New Jersey and park in front of a lovely stone house with a beautiful front yard. They walk hand in hand up the flagstone pathway. She is on top of the world. The man rings the bell and just before the door opens, he turns to the love of his life and says, "You wanna straighten up a little bit?"

I slid the card back into the envelope, walked to Sheila's cubicle, and showed it to her. "Get your coat," she said, her voice businesslike, her face unreadable.

We went to the Warwick bar. "Don't talk for a while. Just smoke," she said. Then, as an afterthought, she added, "But you knew I was going to say that, didn'cha, Psychic Secretary."

Across from us in a darkened booth, two co-workers sat, a man and a woman. They had been there for hours because the woman's head was lolling about on her neck as she alternately whispered lubriciously or laughed too heartily at her companion's jokes. We had a clear view under the table, where we could see her rubbing ever higher up his thigh. He began to slump farther down the banquette, fixing his glazed eyes upon her after briefly checking his watch. A busboy appeared to clear their glasses, and without looking at him, the man said:

"Dos más."

At worst, the insult had been an unwitting one. My boss had chosen to focus on the compliment implicit in "amazing" and "psychic," while all I could see was that other word. And though I thought I might never get out, that I might be taking dictation forever, I knew it would never be as bad as standing, invisible, while some asshole barked orders at me in badly pronounced Spanish.

Sheila and I held our breath as we watched the woman's hand finally make contact with the man's crotch. They had stopped talking altogether and merely looked at one another blearily.

As Warwick regulars ourselves, we were no strangers to this brand of inebriated, abject carnality. But these two were a little bit early, fumbling around as they did so close to Thanksgiving. They might have waited a few weeks for the holidays to start in earnest, when there is no nicer way to say you care than with an under-the-table extramarital hand job.

Those three weeks or so of midtown Manhattan Christmas are an assistant's dream. No work gets done, and all is romanticized melancholy. It was precisely why so many of us had moved to the city, so that we, too, could walk through our antiseptic corporate lobbies, gaze misanthropically at the wreaths adorning the travertine walls, the Christmas tree surrounded with gift-wrapped empty boxes that fooled nobody (and often in the corner, as a concession to our Hebrew colleagues, a cheap tin menorah), and in the fluorescent-lit sadness of it all feel something approaching . . . depth?

Our bosses largely away on holiday, the phones idle, we spent our days going to the movies during lunch, returning hours later to troll the halls of the office, foraging through the gift baskets like a pack of gophers (gofers), subsisting on Carr's water biscuits, individually red-wax-dipped balls of baby gouda, giant cashews, butternut toffee popcorn, smokehouse almonds, and fancy fruit preserves eaten directly from the jar. A diet that had our faces peppered with blackheads and glistening with oily sebum as unto the shining visages of the apostles. In the evenings there were parties, both personal and business, for other publishers, magazines, all of them overflowing with free drink.

Dos Más had nothing on us. Limbs were stroked, kisses were had, bodies were rubbed, people we hardly knew—in kitchens with the lights out—interrupted intermittently for the opening of the fridge door for a beer; in darkened rooms on piles of coats, one or two of which would invariably need to be retrieved midclutch, with sheepish, whispered apology; in the backs of cabs, hurtling drunkenly toward one or the other's home, "the meter glaring like a moral owl," to quote Elizabeth Bishop, ticking away money we could ill afford. *This* was the true spirit of Christmas, boys and girls.

A few weeks into my Psychic Secretary—hood, I sat in a movie theater packed to the rafters. Just before the lights went down, a woman marched up the aisle, looked at me, and asked: "Is that seat taken?"

I was nowhere near the end of the row, but trying to be helpful, I asked, "Which seat?"

Looking directly into my eyes, she said: "That seat." She pointed. She was pointing to the center of my chest.

"Well . . . *I'm* sitting here," I finally managed.

As if I were her college-age daughter who had suddenly announced that I was a vegetarian, she shrugged in a kind of "suit yourself" indulgence of my fantasy of existence and moved on. I looked up and down the row for some sort of laughter, some eye-rolling commiseration, or just plain corroboration that this had just happened, but I got no response. To this day I cannot explain it. Was this an emissary sent from on high at that time of year, not to trumpet the birth of the son of God, but to proclaim with heavenly proof my complete and utter insignificance? She's right, I thought. This seat isn't taken. It was the perfect moment for that time in my life. I mean that, of course, in the worst way possible.

The theater went dark. Up on the screen the camera zoomed past a huge close-up of the Statue of Liberty, swooping down to find the Staten Island ferry scudding along the water, transporting our Working Girl to her office job, where we already knew she would triumph, vanquish the harpy boss, and win the love of the man.

Sheila taught me a survival technique for getting through seemingly intolerable situations—boring lunches, stern lectures on attitude or time management, those necessary breakup conversations, and the like: maintaining eye contact, keep your face inscrutable and masklike, with the faintest hint at a Gioconda smile. Keep this up as long as you possibly can, and just as you feel you are about to crack and take a letter opener and plunge it into someone's neck, fold your hands in your lap, one nestled inside the other, like those of a supplicant in a priory. Now, with the index finger of your inner hand,

write on the palm of the other, very discreetly and unde-
tectably, "I hate you. I hate you. I hate you . . ." over and over
again as you pretend to listen. You will find that this brings a
spontaneous look of interest and pleased engagement to your
countenance. Continue and repeat as necessary.

In the dark of the theater, I write my message, pressing hard
into the flesh of my hand. Although I don't know who I'm writing to, I'm just glad to feel that it hurts.

BEFORE & AFTER SCIENCE

King Constantine II, the deposed monarch of Greece, was passionate about my French vanilla root beer floats. The French vanilla was definitely one of our better flavors; we charged five cents more per scoop. It was completely reasonable that this crowned head of Europe, with his highly developed taste for the finer things, would insist upon nothing less and insist upon no one but me to make them. This is my boxing Hemingway, my wooing Josephine Baker in a swan-shaped bed.

Not every ice-cream parlor in Toronto in the summer of 1982 came equipped with lapsed royalty. But Athos and Melina, the married couple who owned the shop where I worked, were old friends of the king. He spent his time at the front table, chatting with them in Greek, reminiscing about the good times, back when he was still ensconced in happy figurehead-hood, and when Athos and Melina were clearly at the tippy top of Athenian society, he a drug company executive, she a noted scientist in the perfume industry.

They remembered fondly those halcyon days before Constantine's reign, however titular, was effectively ended by an outbreak of democracy. Before he threw his lot in with the slim ranks of perpetually tanned do-little European ex-royals, that shallow band of frivolous hemophiliacs who live out their days reading the yachting news, roaming the world, and dressing for dinner.

Athos and Melina had not been quite as leisurely in their travels. The sense one got was that this was a couple on the lam for some reason. From Athens they had fled to the Sudan, where they continued their rarefied lifestyle and where, a few years later, the volatile politics of that region would send them into flight yet again. Landing them in Toronto, exhausted and vaguely punch drunk, the stunned franchisees of a well-known ice-cream parlor that trafficked in an ersatz Barbary Coast saloon chic of faux Tiffany lamps, frosted mirrors, and wrought-iron chairs. It was an aesthetic so relentless and so forced in its attempt to evoke those bygone days in the City by the Bay that it even went so far as to name its biggest and most vulgar sundae after a civic disaster where thousands upon thousands of San Franciscans were killed. *I know a special birthday boy. Will you be having the Earthquake?*

Imagine, if you will, the queen of France who, instead of succumbing to the decapitory charms of the guillotine, is safely spirited away from France to England, along with other fortunate aristocrats. Now resettled, she runs a fish-and-chips stand in Brighton, where daily the tiny golden ship perched in the frothy waves of her high, powdered wig regularly topples into the deep-fat fryer. This will give you a sense of how profoundly strange was Athos and Melina's presence in our midst.

Athos looked like a latter-day Jean-Paul Belmondo, a formerly handsome man whose features have gone rubbery and heavy with age. He wore dress shirts and socks of the thinnest material I had ever seen. It would be years later before I would recognize these garments of dragonfly wings as the haberdashery of choice of the strip club bouncer, the penny-ante henchman, and the double-breasted thug. But to me, at that time, they indicated only his good breeding. He was, for the most part, a surly, taciturn man, constantly trying to bilk us out of our near minimum wages by pretending to suddenly understand less English than he actually did. But despite his gruff manner, Y chromosome, and ultimate control of our salaries, it was no secret who was truly in charge: Melina. Formidable, fire-hydrant-size Melina. If *she* had ever decided to withhold our payment, she would never have resorted to falsely broken English. She would have simply told us outright, and nobody, not the Royal Canadian Mounted Police, nobody, could have gotten our money out of her. I adored her. She was smart as a whip, was possessed of an appreciative and often bawdy sense of humor, and sounded not a little bit like Peter Lorre. She was also prone to moods so changeable—from borderline-inappropriate affection to homicidal seething rage in mere seconds— that one gave up trying to guess her mental state and surrendered to the hurricane of emotion that was Melina. Sometimes she simply abandoned decorum, as when wondering aloud, the store full of people, "Why do the blacks always order the rum raisin? Tell me. Is it the rum?" Or she might take a sudden dislike to a customer she found stupid: "Madam. You see before you two tubs of ice cream. One is brown and one is purple. There are two nameplates on the glass in front of them. So tell me, madam, HOW IS IT POSSIBLE THAT ONLY ONE OF THESE FLAVORS IN FRONT OF YOU WOULD BE NAMED CHOCOLATE FUDGE BROWNIE BLACKBERRY SHERBET?!? Hmmm? Use your head, madam, please."

While Melina might have yelled at customers with impunity, I have no recollection of her yelling at Athos. In fact, I

can barely remember them conversing at all beyond their talks
with His Majesty. If you hadn't known that they were actually
married, you might never have guessed it. I thought this chilly
estrangement, like Athos's shirts, was more evidence of some
aristocratic world beyond my comprehension.

Actually, Athos and Melina were not aristocrats. They
were meritocrats. Their position in that world of Levantine
glamour from which they had been lately cast out was earned
by dint of study, expertise, and labor. They definitely knew
the meaning of hard work. If anything, it was this new realm of
pineapple syrup and rainbow jimmies that was not up to the
challenge of them.

Take, for example, the light fare that was served in back.
Sandwiches, potato skins, fried mozzarella sticks, and the like,
all meant to be prepared according to the strict specifications
of a menu book put out by number crunchers. A food service
manual full of directives about the height from which pancake
batter should be poured, the optimum diameter of said pancake, the respective number of slices of processed poultry in
the turkey club, versus the sandwich, versus the platter, and so
on. Food as utilitarian and unimaginative as that served from
the galley of a 747. Most franchisees left their kitchens in the
lugubrious but sufficiently capable hands of a bunch of pot
smokers who, a decade later, would find gainful, bleary-eyed
employment at Kinko's.

Not, however, Athos and Melina. To oversee things, they
hired Benoît, an Alsatian of mercurial and easily affronted dis-
position who arrived each day with a leather carrying case of
his own carbon-bladed kitchen knives. Many was the customer
who ducked in order to avoid an enraged Benoît, who would
emerge regularly from the kitchen, clutching an eleven-inch
Sabatier in his wildly gesticulating fist, to scream at Melina
over one of her cost-cutting measures or a difference of opinion over the finer points of the spicy Buffalo wings with blue

cheese dip. *"J'en ai marre de ce bordel! Je ne peux pas faire la cuisine comme ça!"* Even holding weaponry, he was the unarmed party, thoroughly outmatched by the unmovable force that was Melina. A non-native speaker, she could still out-French him, her words flying like tracer bullets from her mouth. After a few minutes of Gallic fireworks, Benoît would return to the back, bested, seething with rage.

Despite Benoît's pyrotechnics of temperament, the kitchen was still a haven for all of us. As anyone who's ever worked in an ice-cream parlor can tell you, two things end up happening really quickly: you get sick of ice cream almost immediately, and soon thereafter you fall in love with the nitrous oxide used to make the whipped cream. You Heart Whippets. This ardor eventually cools when you realize that it's been weeks since you've been able to subtract simple sums, use an adjective correctly, or spell your own last name. But at the first bloom of narcotic romance, you merely wonder where whippets have been all your life.

We were frequently joined in our daily worship at the nozzle by Melina and Athos's son, Nick. I was desperate to be Nick. In 1982 I was sporting pegged trousers so tight at the ankles that by day's end my feet were numb. I was trying valiantly to look alternative, eccentric. Devo. With my hair in a short-back-and-sides 'do with a long and floppy New Romantic quiff on top, framing a face of such poorly concealed sweetness and naiveté, I looked about as threatening and alternative as a baby poodle—as complicated as one of the ice-cream cones I spent my days scooping.

But Nick! Nick had perfected that epoch's brand of sullen anomie, with his eyelids at the perpetual half-mast of weary disdain, his two-tone spiky hair and tapered jeans. If the front of the store was Athos and Melina's putative living room, where they didn't feel the need to talk to each other except in the presence of company, then the kitchen in back was Nick's

domain, where they almost never ventured. The teenage bedroom of one's dreams, namely, one with a working refrigerator,
a six-foot-tall tank of pressurized mind-altering gas, and a gag-
gle of stoners to laugh at everything you say.

Aside from working the register occasionally, Nick
slouched about curating the music, a seemingly constant running loop of *Big Science* by Laurie Anderson, giving special
play to its hit song, "O Superman," with its obligato of metro-
nomic, aspirating laughter. But his true pride and joy was his
self-published magazine, *Before & After Science.* This was years
prior to the term *'zine* and the widespread use of computers.
Like most every homegrown publication from the Punk/New
Wave heyday of the early 1980s, *Before & After Science* was
a samizdat, cut-and-paste affair of snippets of William
Burroughs, Sex Pistols lyrics, black-and-white checkerboard
backgrounds, lots of ransom note typography, old cheesecake
photographs of women in bullet bras, and the ubiquitous image of that Ska Everyman: the porkpie-hatted Teddy Boy,
limbs akimbo in a crazy running dance. *Before & After Science*
was available for sale at the front of the store at a cost of five dollars for the premiere—and what was to regrettably be the
only—issue.

Still, the pile of magazines provided a welcome counterpoint to the saccharine boosterism that invaded the store that
summer. It was dubbed the Summer of *Annie* by proclamation
of the Head Office, in honor of the release of the musical film
adaptation of the Broadway show. Franchisees had been en-
couraged to invest in *Annie* ice cream, a special tie-in flavor.
Annie ice cream was a noxious combination of strawberry and
marshmallow of such a vile and diabetic coma—inducing nature that it was too cloying even for its target market of little
girls, a demographic not known for its sophisticated palate.
Seven- and eight-year-old angels would skip into the store, all
pigtails and horse love, and the scales would fall from their

eyes as they spied the pink and white of the tubs of *Annie,* seeing them for what they were: blatant marketing; a pernicious
inducement to submit to the patriarchy. These apple-cheeked
youngsters became suddenly hardened and cynical. They
took up smoking right there on line, laughing bitterly like
baby Piafs, derisively ordering Futility Shakes and double
scoops of Alienation Chip.

Available, along with the ice cream, and stacked into a
doomed, unpurchased pyramid, were the *Annie* glasses.
Drinking glasses emblazoned with the movie's logo and the
likeness of Aileen Quinn, the little girl chosen in a nationwide
search to portray the plucky, iris- and pupil-deprived orphan.
Sales of these would benefit local charities. Even this altruism
was not enough to move a single tumbler. Melina employed
her usual insinuating tricks.

"Are you wearing Anaïs Anaïs, madam?" she would coo.
"Ah yes, it's a lovely fragrance. I was one of the chemists who
created it in Paris. . . . Yes, thank you so much. Can I interest
you in one of our *Annie* glasses? Of course, it's for charity. . . .
No? That's perfectly fine. I thank you, madam. Good day."

Wheeling around the instant the door closed, she would
hiss at us, "Did you *see* the jewels dripping off of that woman,
and she could not even buy one *Annie* glass. This is a film directed by John Huston, the man who made *The Maltese Falcon.*
What is wrong with you people?"

We just laughed at her, imitating her anger behind her
back. What I could not have known, at age seventeen, was that
Melina's rages had nothing to do with a lack of appreciation
for cinematic auteurism. I was too young to smell in the shop
air the definite tang of flop sweat. That smell of exertion at
keeping away the wolves of failure. It must have seemed so
foolproof to them: an American ice-cream parlor . . . and so
close to America! And how perfect, too, that summer's thematic undercurrent: the unloved cartoon urchin with her little

mongrel, delivered from abandonment and privation to a life of love and untold riches. What a tale of the New World, what fortunate augury under which to begin one's life fresh, for the third time. Nick's magazine might almost have been the story of their family. Before and After Science. "Before" was their tenure in the reliable field of chemistry, where something as ethereal as fragrance—even a fragrance so indescribably heady and complex that its mysteries could be approximated only with images of women lying by swimming pools as shadows of airplanes passed up and across phallic architecture—could be created through the sober logic of a recipe. "After" was this random, anarchic world of business. A world that was failing them—a mapless, unchartable landscape. Looking back, I can see in the pendulum swings of affect the desperation of a woman running out of ground beneath her feet where she could resettle and start over yet again.

A year later, away at college, I would be sent a small newspaper item, the untold story made only sadder by the clinical dispassion of the clipping. A precipitous disappearance, no forwarding address, thousands of dollars in loans and bills outstanding, a shuttered store with no plans to reopen, a sheriff's department notice of seizure taped to the window.

I often imagine them on an airplane. Athos sleeps. Nick tampers with the smoke detector in the bathroom so he can light up. And there is Melina's face at the small round window. Shielding her eyes against the glass, she stares out into the night, past the blinking wing lights, past the Western edge of the continent, out over the ocean, scanning the horizon for the next piece of dry land.

INCLUDING ONE
CALLED HELL

I will come to know it as the Omega Hug. The woman in the fringed halter top and wraparound skirt set sees someone she knows. Walking across the wide-planked verandah—long limbed as a Modigliani, her skin tanned to a tandooried fare-thee-well, her ankle bracelets of tiny silver bells tintinnabulating—she embraces her friend, eyes closed, a beatific smile on her face, her hand moving slowly and healingly up and down the friend's back. The Omega Hug is long and intense, taking a full half minute to execute, but I will see it countless times over the next three days.

At the moment there is plenty of time to Hug. Some two hundred of us are standing around waiting for Steven Seagal to arrive at the Omega Institute for Holistic Studies, the famed New Age retreat center set in Rhinebeck, New York, among the gently rolling hills of the Hudson Valley. Omega offers hundreds of classes and seminars in a variety of disciplines, including writing workshops led by the likes of Grace Paley. But in large part, Omega usually expends its exquisitely positive energy on a curriculum that includes courses like "Out-of-Body Experiences & Dream Exploration," "The Art of Everyday Ecstasy," and "Women's Sacred Summer Camp." Normally these classes are taught by such reigning superstars of the New Age and spiritual movements as Deepak Chopra. But this Memorial Day weekend, the seminar is titled "Cultivating Compassion and Clarity" and our teacher is none other than Steven Seagal—movie star, aikido master, and, lately, teacher of Tibetan Buddhism.

According to the Omega minivan driver who picked me up at the train station, a nice older Santa type who lives six months of the year in a nudist colony in Florida, this weekend's seminar is quite an occasion, second only to Thich Nhat Hanh, the Vietnamese monk and author who attracts 1,200 attendees. There is some concern that it is Seagal's reputation as an aikido master, as opposed to his fame as a movie star, that will bring out the crazies. "You know," says the driver, "guys who want to be able to say they mixed it up with Steven Seagal." Apparently there is heightened security, although aside from having my name checked on a list once on Friday evening by a bird-boned woman whom I could easily take out with a cough, I am not aware of it.

The head of programming for Omega welcomes us prior to Seagal's arrival. He is impressed with the number of men at the seminar (generally Omega retreats are attended by women in the vast majority). "The customary greeting for a teacher is a slight bow with the hands clasped," he advises us. "And it would be perfectly appropriate to address him as Rinpoche. It means 'Esteemed Sir' in Tibetan, literally 'Precious Jewel.' "

Precious Jewel eventually does arrive some forty-five minutes late. What turns out to be Seagal Standard Time. He is in a large phase, with a bit of the late-model Brando girth about him, a dividend of a long time off from making movies. His narrow eyes, sleek ponytail, and variation on traditional Tibetan attire—an aubergine skirt and saffron-yellow satin jacket—lend him the air of a Mongol potentate. He shambles in, displaying a kind of bewilderment, walking slowly, as if this temporal world were too jarring and suffused with craving and pain for him to absorb just yet.

He begins by asking us three questions: "How many of you have some experience with Buddhism?" Easily half the audience has none. He will have to adjust his dharma talks, the Buddhist teachings of the Way, accordingly. "How many of you have any experience with meditation?" Again, about half of us. And finally he asks, "Did the infamous J.J. ever show up?" A blonde, her platinum mane a carefully styled imitation of postcoital disarray, wearing a wrap skirt and Lycra tank top, raises her hand. "Ah, there you are. I see you, girl," he says.

If we are a monolithic group, it is only in that we are overwhelmingly white. Among the five hundred or so people at Omega this weekend, I will count about three African Americans and five Asians, mainly staff, including the three lovely young Tibetan women who are Seagal's disciples. There are some archetypal New Age Stevie Nicks types decked out in southwestern pot-smoker chic—turquoise jewelry, dangly earrings, flowing skirts, and scarves—who all seem to know one another ("Didn't we meet on the Inner Voyage cruise to Cozumel?" I hear one woman ask another). The healthy contingent of aikido/Seagal devotees from a martial arts studio on Long Island—to a man displaying the thick-necked, wide-assed bulk of the fraternity brother—are here to see a world-recognized martial arts master. Alas, they will be disappointed this weekend because Seagal's inevitable aikido display, while admittedly thrilling (for all his size, he moves like a snake-hipped matador), lasts only about twenty minutes. The rest of the group, myself included, seem to be the unwitting members of the American Gap-oisie. We are eastern seaboard types. Although I am here undercover on assignment, as a Japanese studies major, I fit in rather comfortably with the rest of the vaguely disgruntled seekers who, if not of actual Buddhist leanings, are at least conversant with the Eight-Fold Path. Twenty years ago we would have been readers of Robert Persig. Now we own well-thumbed copies of *The Jew in the Lotus*. We've done yoga. We've been lactose intolerant.

Of course, there are a few people among us who have come solely to see a movie star, like the twenty-one-year-old who is still talking about his Sean Connery—themed bar mitzvah ("He's my role model 'cause he's so cool") and the older man who knows nothing about Buddhism and whose questions are generally along the lines of "Anyone ever tell you you looked like a cross between Robert Taylor and Ray Milland?" and "How many meals do you eat a day?"

(Later on I will see this man talking with two women outside the seminar hall, telling them a joke: "Two psychiatrists pass each other on the street. One says, 'Hello,' and the other says, 'I wonder what you mean by that?' " He goes on to explain the joke—because aren't jokes always better when they're explained?—"See, therapists can't take anything at face value," he says, making little lobster claws with his hands. "They've always got to—"

One of the women cuts him off. "You're on shaky ground here, 'cause my husband was a psychiatrist. I don't need to listen to this." She gets up and walks away.

"I'm sorry."

"Don't say sorry 'cause you're not."

Unable to resist, he says to her retreating form, "I wonder what you mean by that!")

As for the serious followers of Tibetan Buddhism, they see Seagal as their Man in Havana, someone whose visibility in Hollywood is beneficial for publicizing the dharma. Seagal is one of their own, and they are admiring, but not cowed. Fans, clearly, but more than that: fellow travelers.

At the time of the retreat, Seagal had already been on a two-year hiatus from Hollywood due to a growing conflict he feels between his roles as star and Holy Man. "The studios know what they want. Fighting. As I became a lama, I had to establish a line I could not cross," he tells us. (He's apparently made peace with that line since then, crossing it to make a film with the very Buddha-like title *Exit Wounds*.)

The Tibet thing is fairly new in Seagal's repertoire of identities. All I had known or read about him prior to this weekend had located him in a different, albeit now less fashionable, part of Asia, namely Japan. Aikido is a Japanese martial art, and in countless articles about him, Seagal has spoken exhaustively, if not a tad mysteriously, about the many decades he spent over there. Even in the crypto-autobiographical introductory sequence to his first film, *Above the Law,* his character is seen teaching an aikido class in Japanese and speaking fluently. So this recent and precariously trendy embrace of Tibet comes as something of a surprise. According to the Omega catalog, Seagal, a.k.a. Terton Rinpoche, has been formally recognized as a *tulku* (incarnate lama from a past life) by H. H. Penor Rinpoche, head of the Nyingma lineage of Tibetan Buddhism. There is perplexity within the American intelligentsia devoted to the Tibetan cause as to how Seagal earned the title so effortlessly. "I haven't looked into this, but I'm curious as to under what conditions or terms he was accorded this status," says Ganden Thurman, director of special projects at Tibet House in New York. "I'm afraid it troubles me," Thurman adds. "I always wondered at the action heroes he played. He always seems to be the only one who tortures his enemies."

For his part, Seagal frames his involvement with Tibet in much the same way he has described his past possible involvements with things like the CIA and sundry international

cloak-and-dagger operations: semishrouded, covert, and intrinsically unreliable. "I was in a monastery in Kyoto and met
some monks from Tibet who had been tortured by the
Chinese. As I was the only one who had studied herbology,
bone manipulation, and acupuncture, I treated them, and
there was an immediate connection."

It's a familiar trajectory. One day you're a simple bone manipulator, the next you're teaching torture victims how to get
centered. You almost can't swing a reincarnated cat without
hitting someone who's followed just this path. The audience,
completely unbothered by the essential unverifiability of
Seagal's explanation, nods with appreciative understanding;
some people close their eyes and smile, credulously savoring
the moment like a divine chocolate.

"Mealtimes are signaled by three blows on a conch shell," says
the Omega welcome booklet. It's a fairly impressive display of
lung capacity, and the people lying here and there about the
hill outside the dining hall applaud. Can I really be the only
one for whom blowing a conch shell resonates with associations to *Lord of the Flies* and the grisly, horrible death of Piggy?
But blithe decontextualization seems to be the name of the
game here (Inner Voyage cruise, anyone?).

Just as at freshman orientation in college, where the first
person you eat lunch with ends up being the person with
whom you take all your meals for the rest of the week, whether
you like it or not, I am forcibly bonded with Meg, a woman in
her late thirties from Massachusetts. She is the first person to
speak to me at breakfast on Saturday. I ask her what she thinks
of Seagal.

"He's interesting," she says.

"Yes. Counterintuitively so," I reply.

"What's that?"

"It's counter to my intuition. I'm surprised. He's quite smart and funny. It's not what I was expecting."

She rolls her tongue around inside her cheek with a smile. "That's not intuition. That's judgment." She is very pleased with herself. This is what passes for a New Age zinger.

Despite his CIA-Buddhist puffery, the biggest surprise about Steven Seagal is that he is not an idiot—far from it. More often than not, he is, in fact, smart, funny, and eminently entertaining. He is far and away the very best thing about the weekend, and he displays near saintly patience and equanimity in answering three days' worth of frequently whacked-out questions with respect and great good humor.

But he is also chemically, tragically late. As our pedagogical leader, his duties are light, having only to lead us in a morning session from nine to twelve and an afternoon class from two-thirty to five-thirty. Seagal tends to arrive at least an hour into each and stays for only an hour. As the seminar continues, the attrition rate mounts. People switch to other workshops, others simply leave. Those who remain are led through a twice daily stretching routine led by Larry Reynosa, Seagal's main aikido disciple. There is a desperation to these calisthenics. We know that Rinpoche is not in the building, and Reynosa knows we know. The routines are lengthened and repeated. What begins on Saturday morning as a fifteen-minute break between the exercises and Seagal's arrival stretches by Sunday afternoon into three-quarters of an hour. I become quite limber.

When Seagal does lecture, it is usually at the primer level. ("It is the law of cause and effect—also known as karma.") As the weekend continues, he shows that he clearly knows his stuff and is capable of elevating the discourse. ("We look at all phenomena as the miraculous activity of the unfolding of the divine. The only thing that's common is what one makes common by one's impure perception.") Basic or sophisticated, however, what's clear is that Seagal doesn't have a whole lot of lecture in him; after thirty or forty minutes the sessions quickly devolve into Q&A. And, as anyone who has ever been to a film festival, stockholder's meeting, or lecture can tell you, when a room is outfitted with microphones for "Q&A," you will hear precious little of anything resembling an actual "Q." So when the young man at the mike kicks off our weekend with, "I guess I'll share something with the group. I recently took out a personal ad that read 'Pagan Universalist Unitarian Buddhist seeks . . .' " I know this retreat will be no different.

It's both fitting and sadly telling that the weekend's discourse begins with someone talking about a personal ad. Unlike college, where a microphone was always an excuse for someone to either exhort the crowd to meet afterward to discuss alternatives to the arms race, decry American imperialism in El Salvador—or, in the case of Columbia University in the early 1980s, for a tiny Trotskyite named Shirley to get up and spin out a jeremiad in support of "Soviet aggression in any form!"—the questions on this weekend devoted to compassion don't get bogged down with a lot of heavy thinking about others. Only one woman asks Seagal what she should do in the face of hate speech. She hears so much of it, primarily against blacks and gays.

"Well, I'm black and gay, and I'm proud of it," says Seagal. The straight, white audience laughs appreciatively and applauds. Racism eradicated, we move on. I find her at dinner that night and tell her how much I admired her question. She thanks me and tells me that she has switched seminars and gone over to the "Freeing the Fire Within" retreat.

Questions of compassion are now left up to the likes of the woman who says, "We had some lamas visiting down in Charleston, and they led us in a meditation where we took on all the pain in the universe. And I had to stop, because there's so much pain in the universe." To look at her, she seems no worse for wear for shouldering all the suffering of the cosmos. I forget to thank her. Later she will ask, "If we are all one and God is in us, does that mean we are God?" She poses it quizzically, as if she had a question about schedule B on her taxes.

But her questions speak to a larger truth about the Omega crowd. There is great concern for the universe here, with the skein of fate and predestination that enmeshes everything, and this concern affects even the most quotidian decisions and incidents: Meg bought a Lumina because "the Spirit told me to. And also the name. Lumina? Luminous?" ("Wait a sec! Lumina *does* sound just like Luminous! My God, do the executives at Chevy know about this?") Behind me in the lunch line, a young woman tells her friends, "So I started to think, Am I gonna hear another song about angels tonight? And I turned on the radio and that song 'On the Wings of Love' came on. And you know the first verse is all about an angel, and I was like, I definitely did not plan this. This is so random. And *then* I thought, Maybe it's not so random."

Another time, a statuesque Susannah York type, a participant in the "Healing the Light Body" shamanic workshop, rolls her eyes back into her head rapturously during our morning meal. "You know, yesterday I *prayed* for organic yogurt, and here it is. It's a manifestation!" she says, her voice breathy and awestruck at the mysterious ways of the Breakfast Deity.

But if things are habitually attributed to higher causes, I am hard-pressed to see them redound to higher purposes. I hear a lot of talk about the good karma accrued by being good to oneself, but actual hands-on altruism gets almost no play the entire weekend. When I wonder aloud how, at a weekend devoted to the notion of *bodhicitta* (awakened compassion), it seems curious that there is no newspaper for us to monitor the suffering of the world at large, Meg tells me, "It's karma." Meaning, I suppose, that those pesky ethnic Albanians—who that very weekend were being slaughtered—were getting what they deserved. "Besides," she continues, "you should take a break from all that." I counter that the casualties of the globe's misfortunes, the purported objects of our compassion, like the Kosovars, don't have the luxury of taking a break. Meg immediately holds up her hands in a frightened Stop gesture. "I was told I just gotta say things, so I'll say that this gives me agita? When things get heavy, I can't eat? Can we talk about something else?"

Meg's reaction turns out not to be all that aberrant. The word I most overhear, flying from mouths like spittle, is "intense." But it usually seems to apply to a massage or a movement class. When I do chance to overhear of a true test of faith and character, one person telling another, "My father died last Christmas and it was fairly intense, so I went to a bereavement workshop, which helped a lot," the response she gets is, "Yeah, when everyone in the room is facing the same direction and the energy is aligned, it can be a very powerful force."

The subject of Tibet itself, origin of the weekend's teachings, is dispensed with in three minutes. A man stands up at the mike and mentions that he heard that the "purpose" of the oppression by the Chinese is so that attention would be paid to Tibetan Buddhism by the world at large. A kind of genocidal PR campaign, ordained by karma: Hitler wore khakis. He relays this information as though he were passing on a handy stain-removal tip.

Even the political T-shirt, that ubiquitous (non-dairy) manifestation of principle, is completely absent, unless a teal garment with the words "Susan B. Anthony" scripted in glitter puff-paint counts. And it's certainly not because of any text-free clothing policy at Omega. I see endorsements for blue-green algae ("food of champions"), Kiss My Face lotion, several polar bears, and an embarrassment of angels (how random, then again . . . maybe not). The only shirt concerned with others is focused on a demographic so remote as to be politically negligible: "U.F.O.ria."

Physically, Omega resembles nothing so much as a kibbutz. Intensely green and lovely, its architecture utilitarian and simple, serving everyone. And if relentless navel gazing and self-obsession, practiced simultaneously by very large groups of people, somehow equaled communalism, then it *would* be a kibbutz. Aside from a rather involved busing procedure in the dining hall of having to separate our dishes, cutlery, and compostable and noncompostable trash, the heavy lifting is left up to the young, pierced, dewy, and eminently fuckable staff.

Reading further in my welcome booklet, I see that the Omega Garden is "[b]ased on the raised-bed French intensive method of gardening [and] is the source of many of the vegetables we serve in the Cafe." This is probably true; it may be a "source," but it's doubtful that it's the bulk, given the garden's jewel-box size and its hypercosmetic rows of nascent lettuces. It's like being told that Marie Antoinette's milkmaid routine kept Versailles in cheese.

A week prior to my arrival at Omega, I was in Disney World with my friend Sarah, where the people on staff are referred to as "cast members"; where we walked from an animatronic display of this nation's presidents to a simulacrum of Tom Sawyer's island in under one minute; where, in the middle of lunching on our "Patriot Platter" in the Liberty Tree Tavern, we were visited at table by Goofy, Minnie Mouse, Chip, *and* Dale. Yet it all felt less ersatz than the faux Arcadianism of Omega. There is nothing wrong, I keep trying to tell myself, with people finding relaxation any way they want. Perhaps there is even something to admire in seeking higher truths in one's spare time. I certainly manage, over the course of the retreat, to have many interesting conversations about Buddhism with many delightful people. Why, then, as I sit in an Adirondack chair under the spreading boughs of a majestic pine tree, a bed of orange poppies beside me, a brook babbling not ten feet away, do I feel as though I am trapped in hell? Funnily enough, Seagal had described hell as being when "you're put in a place where everyone has the same delusion."

The collective delusion here is overwhelming narcissism posing as altruism. I have ended up for the weekend at a spa that refuses to call itself a spa; an "institute" with a terror of the world so crippling as to have no newspapers. No surprise, really, had I but taken the time, prior to my arrival, to seriously parse the terms "self-help" and "retreat." The former unabashedly egocentric, the latter alluding to defeated flight.

The evening's concerts are held in the Lake Theater, a barnlike structure with a small stage. The overhead light is grimy and yellow and flickering as moths and June bugs ping against the bulbs like rice at a wedding. A young folksinger on guitar and piano is accompanied by her ponytailed husband on bass. The audience is sparse, mostly women, alone and in pairs, the demographic hinted at on the first day. They sit with the studied serenity, the composed posture, that broadcasts for all the world to see "I go to things all the time alone. I don't mind."

In Edith Wharton's *House of Mirth,* the heroine Lily Bart—no longer as young as she once was, the financial promises made to her failing to pan out, her prospects at marriage dwindling daily, has a friend named Gerty Farish. Gerty is also unmarried. Gerty has no annuity. Gerty takes her meals in public dining rooms with other single women. And she does so goodnaturedly. Every time Lily sees Gerty, she experiences an interval of panic. Wharton writes: ". . . the restrictions of Gerty's life, which had once had the charm of contrast, now reminded [Lily] too painfully of the limits to which her own existence was shrinking."

After a day of angry, dismissive contempt, the blood beats behind my eyes with identification. I am uncoupled by this unexpected Gerty Farish moment in this crowd of women trying to make sense of a world that has ruled them out of hand for the cardinal sin of having dared to remain single past the age of thirty-five. I have sat alone in theaters, restaurants, parks, my back straight, a book, perhaps. I am acquainted with this good posture.

At one point the singer looks over at her husband and they give each other a smile of such amiable companionship, a look of such pleased and secure partnership, that it reaches all of us with the cold immediacy of a slap in the face. It turns out to be true: when everyone in the room is facing the same direction and the energy is aligned, it can be a very powerful force.

By Sunday morning the hall is decidedly sparser—easily one-half of the people are gone or have decided to opt out of poor Larry Reynosa's relentlessly frequent stretching exercise. There is a picked-over feeling in the room. A buffet down to its garnishes on a soiled tablecloth. "Something very exciting better happen today," says the couple beside me.

Rinpoche certainly tries. We are told he will lead a special fire ritual that morning in honor of the auspicious full moon. But he is late. As we congregate on the lawn in the hot sun, our numbers dwindle yet further. The ceremony, when he finally begins it, is impressive. A smoldering brazier of pine branches and burning pieces of red and yellow cloth sends a plume of thick white smoke up into the summer sky. Seagal chants the Tibetan verses, which he reads from texts bound up in a beautiful silk and lacquer reticule. The English translation is poetry of exquisite intricacy and refraction, speaking of unknowable worlds of bliss and terror—"The five realms of existence, including one called Hell"—unchartable beauties, nuances beyond our conscious comprehension. We are chastened into silent thought.

Arriving at the dining hall that night, we are informed that there will be an unprecedented evening session. I tell Meg that it smacks vaguely of eleventh-hour bang for the buck. Seagal is trying to make up for his "punctuality issues." I say this lightly. Meg, whom at this point I would almost sooner saw my tongue off with a plastic knife than have another one-on-one conversation with, says, "Maybe it's *our* issue. I view this time as a bubble. Maybe we should go with the flow like we're in a monastery." Unable to bear it any longer, I say, my voice far sharper than I intended: "Even in a Buddhist monastery— where I've been"—a bald-faced lie—"they show up at the time they say they will. I don't think it's invalid, having told two hundred people he'd be here at a certain time, for him to show up then."

I frankly don't care whether Rinpoche shows up at all. I am at this point thinking only about the next day, when I can take a cab to the Amtrak station and return to that nest of perversion and unenlightenment known as New York City, where the practice (and criminal nonpractice) of empathy and compassion has all the immediacy, importance, and conflicting allegiances of war.

Meg and I are so clearly sick of each other that her attempt at jocularity merely highlights, rather than defuses, her anger at me. "Wait, let me back up," she says, leaning over toward me with strained Lotus Eater levity, assuming my position in my chair. "Let me learn nonresistance and try to align myself with you." The corners of her eyes are shining, as sharp and gleaming as rat teeth. It's moot, as it turns out, because by the time supper is over we are told that the evening session is canceled.

Disencumbered and disenfranchised, our evening suddenly stretching before us, we start to gather aimlessly in front of the Omega café. Larry Reynosa, who has so far addressed us in traditional Japanese martial arts garb, is there in street drag. A few of the seminarians are asking him questions about his life with Rinpoche. The crowd begins to grow, and a de facto evening session led (not surprisingly) by Reynosa begins to organically take shape in the gathering dusk.

On the periphery of the circle, I begin to speak with an older man whom I noticed earlier. "I'm here 'cause my son did a good job on my taxes and I thought I'd treat him to a weekend." He is dressed in head-to-toe Early Bird Special: athletic shoes with white tennis socks, shorts, Izod shirt snowed with dandruff, and nylon jacket. He has always been a bit of a seeker, he's studying Cabala in Philadelphia. I ask him what he thinks of this weekend.

"It's okay." He shrugs resignedly. "But I didn't really sign on to spend twenty-five hours a day with him," he says, indicating Reynosa.

He is a CPA who refuses to use a calculator. He is delighted when I tell him I'm a writer. "Oh, that must be the most wonderful thing in the whole world! That guy, what's his name . . . James Michener wrote that book *The Drifters,* and I read it at age forty and I freaked out. I'm sixty-six now and I thought, If they can do it, why can't I? And I disappeared for a few years."

"Where did you go?" I ask.

"Aw, I dunno." He sighs, suddenly tired at what a long, strange trip it's been.

The son is as painfully thin as his father, but weak chinned. At least the latter, despite the alpine levels of dandruff and wickedly long eyebrows, still maintains a Martin Landau handsomeness. We decide to head over together to the evening's concert. Tonight it's a woman advertised on the flyers pinned up here and there as having "a voice like dark chocolate." Her tones are not uncocoalike. She sings a lot of noodly Thelonious Monk numbers to which she wrote her own lyrics. In one couplet she innovatively rhymes "just gotta let loose" with "rhythm'll make your body loose." Most noteworthy is her earnest, unsmiling quality; even when she smiles she looks serious: Doris Day at Bennington.

Walking back together from the Lake Theater, we run into a friend of his, also an older Tennis Jew: silver hair, gold chain, athletic wear, tan.

"So what was today like?" he asks. "You and my wife doing the same *farschtunkener chazerai* with the exercise?" Taking his leave, he tells us he is off to the Omega sauna for a *schvitz.*

The moon is a huge yellow headlight as I walk back to my room alone. I stop to look. An older woman with an ice cream walks by, and I point. She stops for a moment and then, putting a hand between my shoulder blades, says, "Thank you." Her hand is comfortingly warm; I hadn't even realized I was cold before she touched me. I sit, moments later, on a lawn chair in front of my cabin, looking up at the stars. Schmuck! I think. Where was this serenity and openness and relaxation three days ago? But I don't really feel serene, relaxed, or open. What I feel is relief at the impending end of this very difficult, singularly lonely experience. (I will find when my phone bill arrives the following month, over the three days, I checked my messages thirty times. It being a holiday weekend, I received not one call.)

Seagal, expected at nine A.M., arrives at eleven forty-five for our final session. The entire seminar is ending at noon that very day. "Is everybody getting hungry?" he asks the clearly had-it-up-to-here crowd. A young man appears at the mike, unilaterally deciding to start the Q&A early. "We were wondering where you were last night and why you're late today.

It's kind of funny and I'm kind of nervous asking, but we're wondering about the mutual respect thing you keep talking about and why you show up for one hour of these three-hour things."

Seagal's face is unreadable as he answers, neither defensive nor angry. "I was told about the eight P.M. session last night as I was leaving. I've been teaching for thirty years and I've never taught as much as I taught yesterday and it comes to a point of diminishing returns as to what you can absorb. I would be happy to give you your money back and a bonus." He then adds a tad tersely, "In my tradition, teachers don't explain. I'm not here to take your money. I'm not flippant about people's time and energy, and I'm very respectful to everyone."

Immediately mollified about the taking of their money and the disrespect shown by Seagal's flippant disregard of their time and energy, the audience applauds. The man thanks him for his very direct answer and sits down.

Meg, seeking to calm yet further the now glass-smooth waters, stands up at the mike. "I've been thinking about the chocolate cake that my friend [Not me, I hasten to point out. Someone else] and I have been eating every night in the café?" she upspeaks. "It's sold in such small slices because it's very rich? What we get here is very rich?" She sits down.

Seagal assumes a demeanor of aching humility for the concluding few minutes of the seminar. He asks in the oblique and roundabout grammatical construction of translated Japanese if it might be all right if he were to possibly read for us a Tibetan prayer called "Inexpressible Confession." "Would that be okay?" he mewls. Yes! we answer, collective tantrum subsided, triumphantly forgiving and eager for dharma enlightenment once more.

But I leave as he starts in on chanting the Tibetan. My taxi is here to take me to the train station. It is a scorcher of a Memorial Day, and as the cab drives away, the vinyl of the car seat burns the backs of my thighs. I am grateful for this small introduction back to *samsara*—the ocean of suffering, the endless cycle of life, death, and misery that is our world of pain. Cracking a window, I lean back and close my eyes, happy to breathe the stifling air.

LATHER, RINSE, REPEAT

Within the canon of anthropological apocrypha—you know, those mythic studies about cultures with fifty ways of saying "mackerel" but no word for "love"—there's that old saw about the underlying proportions of the ideal female form being the same the world over, regardless of epoch or region; the Venus of Willendorf is to Cindy Crawford is to a lovely young bride in Micronesia is to the paragon of Inuit beauty, and on and on.

The woman running through her lines right now is walking, universal perfection. She is lung-collapsingly, jaw-achingly, fall-down-on-the-sidewalk-teeth-first-take-a-bottle-of-pills-and-throw-yourself-out-a-window beautiful. The planes and angles of her face are a mathematical equation adding up to a great cosmic Yes. She's hardly alone in her beauty, in this rehearsal room of a major soap opera called, for the sake of discretion, *Lather, Rinse, Repeat.*

Pretty well everyone here is beautiful. Even the older actors are finely preserved and good-looking, all silver birch and beaten gold, except perhaps for the oldest woman, who has a dowager's hump and has been on the show for decades, since it started as a radio drama, when that sort of thing was beside the point. But the younger actors are the kind of people one generally sees rendered in oils on the covers of paperback novels, locked in heated, semiclad embrace beneath foil letters, as huge antebellum plantation houses burn in the background. That's a lot of roiling passion at seven A.M. Passion from which I am intrinsically excluded. I am decidedly out of my visual league here. To pretend otherwise would be self-deluded folly. In the land of the blind, the one-eyed man may well be king, but in the land of the incredibly beautiful and sighted, the one-eyed man is deformed and ugly.

In the American pulchritocracy—this society ruled by the Beautiful, a term coined by the writer Mark O'Donnell—being on *Lather, Rinse, Repeat* is equivalent to being presented at Court. Daytime Court. I know that there are millions of people across the country who might literally give their lives to be where I am right now, meeting these actors, this aristocracy of a kingdom I know nothing about; a fabled land where the men are shirtless and the women's hair swoops with the sculpted undulations of a Mister Softee. A magical place known as (I think) Pine Bluff.

Everyone has told me both their real and character names. However, having never seen the show nor having read the script (tried to; physically unable), I'm not entirely sure which is which, although it's not hard to figure out when someone says, "Hi, I'm Janet, I mean Crystal."

I am playing a two-day part on *Lather, Rinse, Repeat.* I do not make my living as an actor—it's a hobby. On the rare occasions when I find myself at an audition, it is generally to play one of two character archetypes: Jewy McHebrew or Fudgy McPacker. Jewy McHebrew is usually a fast-talking-yet-beset-with-concern Talmudic sort, whose rapid-fire delivery, questioning answers, and dentated final consonants speak to the intellectual grappling and general worry that is so characteristic of the Chosen People, the People of the Book. Jewy gets to say things like "Papa, I can't believe it. You sold the store?" or "And so we eat the bitter herbs? Why? Becauuuse, it is to remember the bitterness of our enslavement in Egypt!"

Fudgy, on the other hand, can be many people: there is the phlegmatically imperious, supercilious salesman/concierge/executive assistant, who generally has lines like "We're not carrying that this season, I'm sorry. Next!" There's also best friend/next-door neighbor Fudgy, who is forever barging in to display his laughable sexuality by, say, wearing a Carmen Miranda hat, when he's not dispensing clear-eyed advice on matters of the heart. He is America's sweetheart; a harmless queen the whole country can love, with his constant refrains of "Did someone say swim team?" or "Can't you see that he's in love with you, kiddo? Just tell him."

There are, of course, hybrids and permutations. Today's part, for example, is a little bit of Secular Humanist Jewy McHebrew crossed with Cell Phone Schmuck Jewy McHebrew. I am playing, in short, an agent. A powerful New York modeling agent. Let's call him Len Rosenfeld. I am friendly but slick; a hard-nosed businessman with an eye and a taste for beautiful women. Yes, women, thank you very much. Fudgy McPacker has left the building.

"Oh, Tawny," says the International Symbol for Beautiful, making vague washing motions with her hands. "I'll get you for this, if it's the last. Thing. I. Do." It is as if she has raided a Botox dispensary, so unmovable is her perfect face, so uninflected her voice and manner. The director interrupts and suggests as gently as possible that the lines seem to indicate a certain anger and frustration on the part of her character. And, inasmuch as acting is often reductively defined as taking a situation, not in point of fact actually true, and pretending as if it were indeed happening at that very moment, that perhaps she might think of trying a little bit of artifice and simulation when eventually the cameras rolled that afternoon.

"What*ever,*" she hisses, rolling her extraordinary violet eyes as she walks away.

There are two other day principals aside from myself. One is an unspeakably handsome man with a sharp and beautifully gunmetal-blue jaw. The other is an actor I've heard of and even seen on stage. He is playing a preacher. Fifteen years ago, while he was starring in a hit musical on Broadway, his costar apparently said to a friend of mine at a party, "Don't put coke on your dick, man. It's a total waste, it doesn't work."

I, Len Rosenfeld, am just passing through this sleepy bedroom community. I happen upon a charity fashion show, being staged to raise money for the church, which has burned down under mysterious, possibly racially motivated circumstances. Although Len has never been on the show before, he is recognized by the grande dame of the town as if he were a frequent visitor. Apparently I never miss a chance to check out what's happening couture-wise in Pine Bluff.

The extras are almost all seniors, and they almost all seem to know one another. It becomes clear over the course of the long day that doing extra work for the soaps is actually a kind of club. A way for older New Yorkers to get out of the house, be around people, make a little extra cash. It can't be for the amenities, because the soaps, unlike prime time, are decidedly Spartan. I am wearing my own clothes. They pay you ten extra dollars if you bring your own costume. It is the first time that I have acted on camera with my house keys on my person. Even the divas who have been on the show for decades, who have millions of fans, have the same cinder-block-walled dressing rooms as everyone else. They even have to use the same bathroom down the hall.

Moreover, there isn't a cracker to be had on the set. In my limited experience, you can barely walk ten feet at a successful sitcom or on a movie set without upsetting some *étagère* of baked goods and bottled water, or a mandala of shrimp and baby lamb chops. The food deprivation here makes for a lot of low blood sugar among our seniors, which in turn makes them a somewhat unruly mob. Despite an assistant director having shouted, "Quiet, please. Rolling!" one woman has forgotten to turn off the cell phone in her tote bag, which she has brought onto the set. The phone rings in the middle of a scene taking place not fifty feet away. And she takes the call! No one stops her. Indeed, with more than sixty pages of script to film, cut, and print every single day, albeit only on videotape, there isn't a whole lot of room for retakes. *Lather, Rinse, Repeat* is a rude, snuffling beast of barely controlled anarchy, so some old bag chatting with her best girlfriend is hardly the kind of thing that rates starting over. Later on, when I actually tune in to watch my episodes, I see more than one occasion where it's clear that what is being broadcast is a rehearsal take: a woman fucks up her line, literally saying the opposite of what she needs to, then backtracks and rephrases it three times. A man, getting up from behind his desk, slams his leg into the side of it and, wincing, lets out an injured "Unh!" before continuing with his line, which he stammers out in a barely coherent, aphasic approximation due to the extreme pain.

The fashion show begins. The description of every single outfit contains at least one word that the actor—the town's silver-haired patriarch and the fashion show's emcee—has never seen before. "Is it *bow*-dice, or *baw*-dice?" I volunteer as how I think it's *baw*-dice. "What's this? Pail . . . pail . . . ?"

"Paillettes," I tell him. "They're like sequins."

"Do you actually work in fashion?" he asks me in all seriousness.

My character is unmoved by the proceedings on this podunk runway (I'm not bowled over my real self, either, not being terribly fond of teal or shell pink) until of course I see Mimi, the show's tragic mulatto. The camera sees me see her. I make a note in my program. My look is interested and coolly appraising with an underlying vulpine, frankly sexual quality. I'm impressed. And remember, please, I am a big deal. The urbane toast of the Big Apple, pulling down a high-six-figure salary, living in an extra-ritzy penthouse apartment, I am sure. I am a man not in the habit of having my insatiable, voracious appetite for the finer things in life—chilled baby duck, sushi, chocolate-dipped strawberries, and beautiful women—going unsatisfied. So when I say to Mimi that I think she has an "absolutely fantastic look," that I am stunned by her style and the way she wears a dress, that I think I could make her very, very rich, and that I would like more than anything to get her up on the runway at a small but quite important show I'm planning in New York City the following week, and she says no thanks, she's perfectly happy to use her modeling talents only for good, in the name of social justice and the refurbishment of the House of God . . . I am a little taken aback, to say the least. It only serves to pique my interest further. Beauty *and* pluck. A tiger to be tamed! I leave her my card, convinced that she will reconsider.

I'm thinking of all the things I will buy with the money that comes rolling in when eventually this subplot continues and Len Rosenfeld is a semiregular character. I've planned it all out: I can see Mimi's argument with her boyfriend that precipitates her tearful flight to New York. Her first tremulous arrival at my atelier-cum-bachelor-pad. She has caught me in the midst of dressing down some weeping supermodel. The mask is definitely off, and I am yelling, "Do you honestly think I would let you do Gregor's show? You don't do anything without my say-so. And you wanna know why, babycakes? Because I own y—" I sense someone behind me. I turn around. I switch faces immediately. "Mimi, isn't it?" I purr, pleased and quietly triumphant. I invite her in, "No, of course it's not a bad time . . . a business discussion. I'm just really glad to see you." I feign surprise to hear that she has nowhere to stay, no friends, no family in town. Conveniently, I have extra room. A great many of my models stay there. Len at this point might even look at her and say something like "Hey, Mimi, *mi casa es su casa.*" She is overwhelmed by my generosity and her good fortune. One of my minions—Kara, let's call her (who, in a later episode, while pressing into Mimi's uncomprehending hands a faded yearbook photograph of the winsome innocent creature that she, Kara, used to be before I used her up, will exhort Mimi to "get out while she still can!" but for now, a narcotized and silent girl)—shows Mimi to one of the guest rooms upstairs. The camera holds on my face as I watch their ascent. I roll my tongue around in my closed mouth as if I were tasting something indescribably sweet and delicious.

Weeks later, when I tune in to watch the show, I see myself give Mimi my card. I see myself urge her to call me, and I see myself leave. And then I watch as Mimi takes my business card in her hand. After studying it briefly, she crumples my Pine Bluff future into a ball and lights it with a match. Like most things made of paper, it burns.

HIDDEN PEOPLE

It is not pleasant to have my bluff so thoroughly called. My idle claim of being a translucent-skinned neurasthenic who cares nothing for sunlight is incontrovertibly shattered after a mere ten minutes of ambling through the duty-free shop at Keflavík airport in Iceland at ten in the morning. The November sky outside is still as dark as four A.M., precisely the time it would be for me if I were still back in New York. But I am not back in New York and should, by all rights, be enjoying that cognitive dissonance that is the happy dividend of transatlantic air travel: the European day, brightly risen and well under way six hours before its time. I find myself existentially, spirit-robbingly sad as I look over the shelves of vacuum-packed salmon, tinned smoked puffin, lumpfish caviar, and licorice, waiting for a ride into Reykjavík. By the time I have been in Iceland for an hour I am a walking Edvard Munch lithograph. All is blackness in my heart as well as outside the windows of the bus during the hour-long trip into town. The vehicle fishtails wildly, buffeted by inhospitable winds. When I get back to New York, I think to myself, I shall never again denigrate the light. I will start a letter-writing campaign to institute National Photosynthesis Day. I will join a tanning salon.

I have come to do a story on Iceland's Hidden People, invisible beings from another dimension who, along with elves and trolls, are a mainstay of the country's folklore. It was a newspaper story about the Hidden People who live in Grásteinn—literally Gray Rock—one of Reykjavík's most renowned boulders, that brought me here. Grásteinn sits, cracked in two, fat and satisfied on its own square of sod just to the side of State Road #1, leading north out of the city, surveying the highway traffic that it has managed to divert not once, but twice.

Viktor Ingolfsson is chief of the publishing unit for the Icelandic Public Roads Administration. He has brought me to the rock. Any and all newsworthy incidents that occur anywhere along Iceland's twelve thousand kilometers of road are Viktor's bailiwick.

Incidents like Grásteinn. In 1971 plans were under way to resurface Road #1, making it necessary to detonate Gray Rock. Suddenly locals came forward and protested the destruction, claiming that it was inhabited. It was claimed that any desecration of the Hidden People's home would result in innumerable and unfathomable bad things. This is nothing new; accounts of construction accidents, malfunctioning equipment, and garden-variety bad luck associated with unheeded warnings have entered the national mythology. So despite no history of Hidden People tales attached to the rock prior to 1971, the Public Roads Administration bowed to the protests and spared the boulder.

In 1999 road expansion necessitated Grásteinn's being moved yet again. By this time the intervening decades had lent the rock a legitimacy, a bona fide national importance. Where originally it had been moved with a big bulldozer and a push—such brusque treatment that resulted in the rock's cracking in two—the photographs that Viktor shows me of the most recent operation show a sling of yellow nylon belts: a rock coddled like an egg.

The pictures of this delicate procedure are in the internal newsletter of the PRA. Viktor puts out two weekly publications—one internal, the other for widespread consumption. The public newsletter made no mention of this second Grásteinn incident.

Viktor has been working for the PRA for thirty years, since his first summer job there as a boy of fourteen. Prior to my arrival, he had sent me an article he had written about the Hidden People sites under the PRA's jurisdiction. It is titled "The Public Roads Administration and the Belief in Elves." It turns out to be quite beautifully written—in addition to his day job, Viktor is a novelist; his third book has been on the national best-seller list for months—and the craft is evident in what, in other hands, would be nothing more than a press release.

The article is a minor classic of shifting tone, a fascinating mixture of weary exasperation and respect for the feelings of others. He writes: ". . . a lot of time goes into answering the same old questions. . . . This text . . . can be looked upon as the author's interpretation of the PRA's view on the issue. It will not answer the question of whether the PRA's employees do or do not believe in elves and 'Hidden People' because opinion differs greatly and it tends to be a rather personal matter. However, you may assume that the author severely doubts the existence of such phenomena." About the alleged curses and tales of accidents surrounding construction, he gently chides the reader, ". . . everybody has their ups and downs in life and we all suffer blows . . . you should ask yourself when was the last time something equally bad happened and who was bothered that time?"

The *New York Times* story that piqued my interest has made Viktor the focus of much foreign attention. If he is sick of being called by reporters (he was very easy to find; the old wives' tale about the Icelandic telephone directory being listed by first names turns out to be completely true), he makes an intermittently good show of hiding it. When I ask him what his other duties as publishing director are, he cheerfully replies, "Oh, I do all sorts of strange things. Like talk to you people." Viktor has offered to show me around some of Reykjavík's enchanted spots. But first, to give me a proper look at the city, we drive up to the Pearl, a huge glass bubble housing a café, revolving restaurant, and an observation deck that sits on a hill above the city. The sphere, which does indeed shimmer like a pearl, is built on top cf the huge cisterns the size of oil tanks that hold the city's hot-water supply. Viktor explains that Reykjavík is heated geothermally, making it the cleanest capital city on earth. "You might smell a little sulfur when you shower. I don't notice it anymore," he tells me. That "slight smell of sulfur" proves to be an almost unbearably nauseating stench for the uninitiated.

The view from atop the Pearl is not what I had expected. I had envisioned a baby Amsterdam, all spun-sugar northern European architecture: spires, gables, cobblestones. Despite being over two hundred years old, it is surprisingly new. It turns out to be a very Bauhaus kind of town with a very low horizon, only a few stories high, and very many of the buildings, houses included, are clad in corrugated metal siding. It looks not a little like a vast Audi dealership.

Getting back into the car on an overcast afternoon, he admits openly that these Hidden People incidents, when they come up, represent a PR problem for the Public Roads Administration. They then have to brace themselves for being labeled as insensitive. There's also the danger that such reports will open the floodgates and all manner of copycat stories will come rushing in, despite the fact that, according to Viktor, very few people actually believe in this quaint folk tradition. If that's so, I wonder aloud, why make any concession?

"Because the people who do believe, they are pretty serious about it," he says.

I counter as how we certainly have people who believe in a lot of things that no one else does and we would never think to listen to them.

He explains Reykjavík's unique situation to me: "This is a small community, you see. So basically everyone knows everyone, almost. You really have to listen to everyone, because you could probably meet them at a party in a little while. When you scream at someone in traffic in New York you know you're not going to meet them again, so you do it, but not so much here."

His reasoning is valid, even if only mathematically. There are arguably as many people within a half-mile radius of my apartment—that's just ten blocks in any direction—as there are in the entire country of Iceland. I am infinitely more tolerant of the psychotic woman with Tourette's syndrome who walks up and down my block all day long every day, starting at six A.M., precisely because I see her every day. Although effectively a complete stranger, she is more than that. She is my neighbor. Plus, she seems to enjoy picking up litter. But that's not the point; the fact is, we all live with daily superstitions, vestiges of ancient beliefs: otherwise completely pragmatic grown-ups who refuse to walk underneath ladders; brief interruptions in conversation while someone scrambles around to find some wood to knock on.

· · ·

Arni Bjornsson is a cultural anthropologist and head of the Ethnological Department at the National Museum. He is a sweet-looking, beetle-browed grandfatherly type. A man in his seventies, originally from a farm in the countryside, he closely mirrors Iceland's emergence into the modern age. Like Viktor, Arni also seems wistfully regretful that the pretext that gets someone like me on a plane and over to Iceland is to scrutinize this daffy, essentially nonrepresentative aspect of a society that is distinguished in countless other ways—the oldest parliament in the world, the legendary consistency of its gene pool, the highest number of published poets per capita on earth. Imagine you are outside a jazz club, a place devoted to a quintessentially American art form, and a reporter from elsewhere comes up and, microphone in hand, starts quizzing you on why so many high-rises here don't have thirteenth floors.

When Arni speaks of his childhood in rural Iceland, he distills very clearly the ambivalent relationship it seems most Icelanders have with these myths. "I didn't believe, but I didn't exclude the possibility. In my own farm there were two cliffs, and it was said that some Hidden People lived there, and you should not cut the grass near the cliffs because it belonged to the Hidden People. There were stories about men who had not obeyed this rule and they had some accidents."

This turns out to be a paradigmatic model, which I hear over and over again: the Story of the Grass Belonging to the Hidden People That Must Never Be Cut; Erma Bombeck "My Husband Is So Lazy . . ." joke as folkloric myth.

The other model of story that keeps coming up is one of benevolent wish fulfillment as opposed to disguised admonition. In these stories, mortal women fall into slumbers from which they cannot be woken. In this dream state they are visited by Hidden People. They are taken into Hidden People's homes, invariably more comfortable than their own, and also invariably, having performed some service or having been fallen in love with, these mortal women are given pieces of fine cloth, much finer than anything available to them in their waking lives.

Hidden People are neither intrinsically malevolent nor are they smaller than human beings. It seems that their seminal differences lie in their concealment and the greater comfort of their hidden lives.

"The Hidden People are like human beings, but if anything, they are more beautiful, they are better clothed. The world of the Hidden People was a sort of dream world for the poor people. They had better houses, furniture, clothes, food. Iceland is a land of contrast. Geologically it is a very young country, glaciers, volcanoes, earthquakes, lava streams, there was no stability. This instability has an effect on national character. When we think that there were practically no towns in Iceland until the nineteenth century, people with vivid fantasies on the individual and very scattered farms, they found themselves neighbors in the nearby cliffs and hills."

Freud's theory of dreams is ultimately that they are, at heart, disguised versions of unacceptable wishes, of infantile desires whose fulfillment is necessarily unhealthy or unattainable. In a country as physically inhospitable as Iceland once was, with its spread-out, sparse population, things as basic as warmth, clothing, sufficient food, and companionship might all be seen as inappropriate eruptions from the id. Despite having been in Reykjavík only a few days, I understand Iceland's particular brand of desolation. In an effort to banish the blues during those few hours between when the sun goes down at about four and the time when it might be appropriate to start drinking, I take myself to see *Fight Club,* which, while featuring an awfully good performance by the four-inch band of flesh across Brad Pitt's stomach just above his pubic hair, does little to lift my spirits.

For the most part, however, the nasty brutishness of the elements in present-day Reykjavík is really no more than a phantom pain. Still, the stories that hearken from that hardscrabble time are fondly remembered and closely guarded by people. Arni cites a study that found that 10 percent of the population firmly believed in Hidden People, 10 percent firmly disbelieved, and the remaining 80 percent hovered somewhere along the continuum of skepticism. This seems fairly well borne out when I talk to people. They can all recall local stories about rocks that must be avoided, grass that must not be cut, construction snafus, and the like. One young woman—a super hip chick in a long black skirt, shiny dark red top, glittery boa, and black felt platform boots—claims to have seen an elf once. When I press her for details, though, she can conjure up little more than the standard Disney details of a beard and a little hat. Interestingly, wherever the people I interview land on the spectrum of credulity, pretty well all of them think that it's at the very least only sporting to make an effort at belief.

It is that yearning quality, that sense that it's at least nice to believe in Hidden People, that comes up again and again, even from a skeptic like Arni. The tales are a vestige of a pre-urban Iceland. They are a holdover from what came before. And the physical record of what came before seems to be disappearing at an alarming rate in Reykjavík. Everywhere I look there is new construction. Urbanization is intrinsically a violent process. It elicits a terrified nostalgia; it makes us want to hold fast to what we feel is being lost: this was at the heart of the Arts and Crafts Movement of the nineteenth century, with its concentration on handiwork, on the nonindustrial; in part it's what made the Brothers Grimm decide to compile their oral ethnography of indigenous German folk tales when they did; even Martha Stewart's monomaniacal obsession with the homemade is born of a similar impulse. An impulse to, if not stop time, at least slow it down some, preserve some sense of history.

To hear Magnus Skarphedinsson tell it, he founded his Elf School in a similar spirit of folkloric anthropology. The school offers four-hour seminars, mostly for foreigners. The course includes a bus tour of the main elf and Hidden People sites in Reykjavík, followed by a typical Icelandic coffee and pancake breakfast. It's all pleasantly low rent. The sign on the door is a paper flyer decorated with a drawing of a cartoon ghost, complete with the sheet on its head and its hands outstretched; some elves building a sweet little house; and a horseman being guided through the night by a hooded spirit, hovering in a nimbus of fire. The Elf School also offers aura readings and past-life explorations. In the hallway outside Magnus's office stands a plaster elf about three feet high. He has a gray beard and a green hat and britches. Garden-variety garden gnome.

Within that 10 percent of people who yearn for Hidden People to exist, Magnus, it seems, yearns the most. But he covers this yearning with a veneer of clinical dispassion. "I'm just a historian. A scientist," he says. He refers to what he sees as a general disbelief as a "dilemma." He is convinced that if similar funding were poured into the scientific research of Hidden People as it is into other areas, like medicine, we would have conclusive proof of their existence. When I ask precisely what specific kind of scientific testing might be addressed, Magnus leaves it at "finding all the dimensions other than our own." Magnus is clearly on the bus, despite his claims of neutrality.

He leads me through the different types of elves. Some are humanoid while some are more simian. They range in size from less than an inch up to just under five feet. Magnus speaks about Hidden People as an anthropologist or census taker might. In contrast with elves, Hidden People are completely human, divisible into three types: those who are about a foot taller than us and dress in ancient Icelandic garb; a little-known group who dress all in blue and are sometimes even blue skinned; and the main population of Hidden People, numbering up to some thirty thousand individuals, who "are totally like us but a little smaller, and their clothing is like ours but about fifty years from the past."

This last detail makes things a little clearer. It can't simply be a matter of fashions taking a generation to penetrate the spirit dimension. I'd like to believe in a world of benevolent and beautiful creatures who live in rocks as much as the next guy, but it seems decidedly to be falling down on one's scientific method job not to inquire more deeply into the fact that the vast majority of Hidden People sightings have them dressed in the clothing of, oh, I don't know, one's dead relatives.

But I cannot help being touched by Magnus's devotion to his subject. Even the contradictions, the lapses in interrogative rigor, are, in the end, not much different from those of someone who has faith in God or a religion. There's something quite sweet about his ardent hope that one day he might be granted some access, that the beings he spends all his days documenting might make themselves visible to him. "Oh, I would love to see them, especially to be invited to the cliffs, and I would ask them five thousand questions." He becomes positively animated as he talks about it, his voice whooping up in excitement. "Where did you get the carpet, where did you get the table, where did you get the stove, have you been abroad?" Recovering his composure, he adds, almost embarrassed, "That's probably the reason they haven't invited me."

It clearly rankles him a little bit that Erla Steffansdottir, a piano teacher and one of Iceland's most noted elf communicators, claims she has been seeing elves and Hidden People her whole life. Magnus has led me to believe that my chances of meeting Erla would be slim to none, that she is a difficult prima donna, that she will not be helpful, that she traffics in arbitrary rivalries within the elf community.

I'm inclined to believe him after my initial encounter when I call to set up the interview. She actually seems to be sobbing uncontrollably on the other end of the line, all the while talking to me. In her defense, who actually picks up the phone in the middle of a crying jag? Besides, without having to push, she tells me to come the next day at four o'clock.

I was expecting wild gray hair, clanking jewelry, a tatterdemalion velvet cape from whose folds wafted the scent of incense, a house full of candles, dream catchers, cats, and bad art. Instead I found a friendly if somewhat shy woman in her forties living in a lovely apartment on the top floor of a Reykjavík town house with a bay window. Aside from a tiny elf figure made of three painted stones, piled up snowman style outside her front door, Erla's house is decorated in the tasteful, middle-class aesthetic one might expect of a piano teacher: landscape paintings, old furniture. The place is warm and cozy on a particularly blustering, windy day.

Erla's friend Bjork is there to translate, although Erla's English is sufficient to slap me down at our rather awkward beginning. I ask when she first realized she could see Hidden People. "This is very stupid to ask when I see. When I was born. Like that one right there," she says, indicating a place on the coffee table beside a Danish-modern glass ashtray. She then catches herself. "Oh, that's right. You can't see it." She shakes her head slightly, amused at her forgetfulness that others do not possess her gift. It's a somewhat disingenuous moment, like when your friend, newly back from a semester in Paris, says to you, "It's like, uhm, oh I forget the English word, how you say . . . *fromage?*"

Apparently the coffee table in front of me is a veritable marketplace of elves milling about, many of them in separate dimensions and oblivious to one another. Bjork takes over, essentially ferrying me through this gnomish cocktail party:

"One sits there, two are walking over here, one sits there. When she plays music they come. It attracts them."

I am suddenly overcome with a completely inappropriate urge: the barely suppressed impulse to slam my hand down on the coffee table really, really hard, right where she's pointing.

Apparently the elves on the table are in too remote a dimension, and are too small to talk to. Conveniently, every home also comes equipped with a house elf, about the size of the average three-year-old, with whom one can communicate. "Every home?" I ask.

"Yes, you have one in your house in New York, too," Bjork assures me.

If only my house elf, sick and tired of my skepticism, was taking pains to prove his existence once and for all by cleaning my apartment for me at that very moment, I joke. Leadest of balloons.

Bjork points out that house elves are a privilege, not a right. When the energy of a given house gets too negative, she says, when there is drinking or fighting, the elves will leave. Not terribly surprisingly, mysticism, New Age philosophy, recovery-speak, and elves are conflated as one. Erla says that elves are a manifestation of nature, they are inherently good; without them we would choke on our own pollution. There is almost no more urban a view of nature than this pastoral, idyllic one: Humankind bad, Nature good. As in, drinking and fighting bad, elves and flowers good. But it's a false dichotomy. After all, following this logic, Sistine chapel bad, Ebola virus good?

· · ·

Over the course of my trip, I visit three inhabited sites. The Gray Rock, another small pile of rocks covered with wintry grass called the Elf Bank Road, and a third place where Magnus takes me: a boulder that decades previously is said to have wrought havoc on egg production at the nearby poultry farm. What's extraordinary about all of them is how visually unprepossessing they are. None have the prototypical look of "enchantment" we might associate with fairy tales. They aren't impressively sized, they are not possessed of anthropomorphic whorls or striations in their surfaces, overhung with gnarled vines. In fact, they are just lichen-covered rocks, resting on yellowing squares of sod. Magnus's aged dog, Tinna, relieves herself no fewer than three times during the short interval we spend at the chicken rock. You can't blame the dog; the rock looks like the perfect place to take a leak, sitting as it does at the end of a very unphotogenic gravel driveway, near a covered garage and a chain-link fence. Aside from a very small plaque that reads "Borka Mynjar," "Place Protected by the City," there is no discernible effort made to beautify the surroundings. Other than not bulldozing them or blowing them up, there seem to be no concessions made for these mystical neighbors.

As for that other type of concession, the kind selling gnome ware, clothing printed with "I was a succubus in a boulder in Reykjavík and all I got was this lousy T-shirt" or stuffed elves, there is none. I see this as a lost opportunity, marketing-wise. In four days in Reykjavík I have seen a total of maybe eight elves, not one of them for sale.

I can't chalk this reserve up to embarrassment. Not everyone has the same concerns as Viktor, hoping to keep reports and stories at a minimum. Even a circus barker like Magnus with his school pulls his punches and sells nothing more pricey than a bus tour and some pancakes. This reserve is almost incomprehensible to a North American, where even the

vague impression of the face of Mother Theresa peeking out of
the pastry folds of a cinnamon bun was enough to turn the coffee shop where it appeared into a shrine, however briefly. It almost seems as though folks are taking their cues from the
Hidden People themselves, respecting their concealment and
according them the peace and quiet of beloved, beleaguered
stars.

On my way out of the city to Keflavík airport I get a sustained
look at the landscape that was dark upon my arrival. In the
weak afternoon light, it is an unrelievedly monochromatic
view: flat, vaguely undulating black rock, cracked all over
with a tracery of fissures. To the right the vast gray sea, and
to the left in the distance the strange hills, looking like
whales resting on their sides, each one isolated against the
horizon. At one point we drive within half a mile of the perfect cone of a young volcano. In the gray sky, the darker gray
curtain of a rainstorm travels back and forth over the land,
over the bus.

In *A Midsummer Night's Dream,* Shakespeare describes the
Athenian wood that lies just beyond the gates of the city as a
place ". . . where the wild thyme blows, Where oxlips and the
nodding violet grows; Quite over-canopied with lush wood-
bine, With sweet musk-roses and eglantine": It's crowded in
that Athenian forest. You can't take two steps without bump-
ing into some confused lover or rude mechanical sporting the
head of an ass. By contrast, Icelanders were frequently all
alone in the wilderness, with no blossom-heavy branches con-
cealing countless magical faeries. The spaces yawn open,
wide, and disconnected. And it is our nature to connect, to
create for ourselves a fully formed community where none exists. We are hardwired for it. As Theseus says:

The poet's eye, in a fine frenzy rolling,
Doth glance from heaven to earth, from earth to heaven;
And, as imagination bodies forth
The forms of things unknown, the poet's pen
Turns them to shapes, and gives to airy nothing
A local habitation and a name.

EXTRAORDINARY ALIEN

There is no welcoming decoration on the walls at the Immigration and Naturalization Service in Manhattan. Nor do the people who work there seem particularly happy to see any of us who have come that morning for our green card interviews.

After the metal detectors and bag check, we are thumbprinted. The woman administering the procedure is suspicious and exasperated by some "highly abnormal striations in the pads of my digits." A Chinese couple is greeted by their lawyer, who is as young and eager as a puppy. He pumps the husband's hand vigorously and then, exuberance unabated, he grabs the wife by the shoulders and kisses her on the cheek. She looks horrified.

I have more in common with the English-speaking Americans working behind the desk. I already work in the United States, and I am American educated. There are even very real differences in my case. My green card comes

through something called the "extraordinary alien" program. A bit of a joke, really, since the only really extraordinary thing about me is my level of access to the writers of
national stature whom I've met through my day job and the
many friends I have who work at prominent magazines and
book publishers with creamy letterhead. All of these people
have provided me with written statements attesting to the
government that I should be allowed to stay in this country. It
is a dossier of connection and privilege. The usual eighteen-
month-to-two-year waiting period for approval was, in my
case, four weeks. Even my eventual green card is different:
"E-1," the highest grade, apparently, although I still have no
idea what that means.

I am a first-generation Canadian. My circumstances did
not necessitate flight, unlike most every generation of my family before me, as well as everyone else in the waiting room. I am
aping the immigrant experience that, for so many here, is a
deadly serious one. After two hours I approach the woman at
the desk, hoping she has by now forgotten my thumbs, and
say, my voice authoritative yet quiet and nonregional, like my
countryman Peter Jennings:

"I'm sorry. I was under the impression that I didn't need
an interview this morning."

It works. I am ushered in immediately. The cubicle of the
young INS employee is smaller than my office. I am approved
and out on the street in ten minutes. As I make my way to the
subway, my heart is like that of my countrywoman Joni
Mitchell: "full and hollow like a cactus tree." Strange, since
with green card in hand—something I had yearned for over
many years with a near physical ache—a lot of my problems
had largely been eliminated. My presence in these United
States was legally secure. Now I could work part-time or not at
all. Up until then, securing and keeping a job was an exercise
in a kind of Blanche DuBois patronage, depending as I did

upon the kindness of my employers not to fire me or rat me out to the feds.

There was also the equal and opposite danger that I might find myself trapped in indentured servitude in a less than ideal situation. I once interviewed for a job assisting a man with whom I knew people in common. Terrifyingly, rather than singing his praises, our mutual friends could only lamely volunteer that he had "conquered a lot of his personal demons" and was now much more in control of his anger. "He still feels bad about throwing that mail meter at his employee's head, and that was years ago!"

His office was also his home. A loft on a busy thoroughfare in SoHo; an airy, open space decorated in an unyielding, hard-edged Helmut Newton, S/M style, with hostile glass-and-black-leather furnishings. The metal legs of all the tables were in the shape of branches barbed with iron thorns. I was to meet him there, and we would talk and then go for supper, for which he would pay. I was at a point in my life when the prospect of a free meal still held real excitement. I wore a suit.

He produced country-western dance revues for theme parks. He had just started taking these shows over to India. As his assistant I would make a living wage, a novelty for me back then. In return, he told me, "You make my life easier. Whatever *that* means!" he snorted.

"These people in India," he continued with laughter, "have *never* seen a C and W show before. Never."

He was a very specific type of man. The type of man who breaks into a noncontextual smile on an isolated word and then turns it off just as quickly. It is a frightening habit that conveys that it is taking all of the speaker's energy, socialization, or neuroleptic medication not to haul off and punch—or throw a mail meter at the head of—the listener for their stupidity. "When we opened last year (*smile*) at Six Flags Benares (*smile*), it was like we were Hindu gods or something."

His assistant of ten years, the fellow I would be replacing, had the unphotosynthesized pallor and stooped gait of some-one who has been living under the basement stairs. He brought in one of their brochures for me to see. In it, clean young men and women in pressed jeans and gingham twirled lariats and danced. They had been captured on film, mid—"Yellow Rose of Texas," smiling wildly, furiously baring both rows of teeth, as if they had been set on fire.

"So, David (*smile*). What do you want to do with your life?" he asked me.

"Well, I haven't really deci—"

"Because, the thing is (*smile*)," he continued, "I'm not really looking for someone who's window-shopping (*smile*) for a career."

I was twenty-three years old at the time. My only power lay in my capacity to say no to men like this. Unsatisfying as my current job was at that time, as I looked around that loft, I saw the clear narrative arc of what my life there would be: from the initial impatient word-processing tutorial, the subsequent paranoid recriminations that I was stealing office supplies (which, of course, would be true), on until the final confronta-tion with him yelling at my retreating, weeping form: "You'll never work in country-western theme park musical revues for South Asian export again!"

So why was I standing here on lower Broadway feeling so *Canadian?* Why now, of all times, this sudden fear of having my essential Canadian-ness erased? I had been on a mission from the day I first came to New York at the age of seventeen to pass for native, but suddenly I felt the need to proclaim my differ-ence.

And we are different, in subtle yet formidable ways. My

countryman Robertson Davies summed it up when he pointed out that the national character of Canadians, such as it is, owes a great deal more to the stoic reserve of Scandinavia—its latitudinal and climatic sister—than it does to the United States.

There are even more galvanizing aspects to the Canadian psyche than mere reticence. There is the collective fear, at least when I was growing up, of becoming too big for our britches. To paraphrase Lorne Michaels (my countryman), it's the kind of place where they award Miss Canada to the runner-up, because the prettiest already gets to be prettiest. Rather than demanding liberty or, failing that, death, we are a country forever giving up our seats to the elderly, all the while thanking one another for not smoking.

Which is not to say that we are raised without national pride; we just think it goeth before a fall. Sometimes, though, we just can't help ourselves. Canadians *always* know who's Canadian. Say "John Kenneth Galbraith," "Kate Nelligan," "Hume Cronyn," "Banting and Best," "the Cowboy Junkies," or "Monty Hall" (facilitator of the deal, that ultimate American art form) to Canadians and watch a flicker cross their eyes like the shadow from an angel's wing. After a polite interval, three seconds or so, they will say, as if an afterthought: "He's Canadian, you know."

And it's not limited to prominent people, either. Those individually wrapped slices of processed orange cheese food are known as Canadian singles (a dubious honor, to be sure). The mechanical arm on the space shuttle used for making interstellar repairs—the Shuttle Remote Manipulator System—is also known as the Canadarm. In fact, the shuttle is never referred to on the Canadian news without its Homeric moniker, as in "The American space shuttle, with its Canadarm . . . blew up today." Indeed, ask Canadians what they think a space shuttle is for and likely as not they will respond, "Oh, to go up into space and move stuff around . . . with an arm."

When I was growing up, families like mine played "Who's Canadian?" with the same all-consuming devotion with which we played "Who's a Jew?" (leaving out Meyer Lansky and the Son of Sam, of course). Can you then imagine the double triumph in the households of my youth in spotting the Canadian Jew? Lorne Greene! You fairly cannot conceive of anyone more heroic than Lorne Greene, nor the crestfallen sadness when people realized that Andrea Martin of SCTV wasn't just not Jewish—she is Armenian—but is from Maine, having just lived in Canada. This was quickly rationalized and Ms. Martin claimed as one of our own with the reasoning "Armenians are very similar, and Maine is very close, and she lived here so long."

We are stealth aliens, like the Communists in the propaganda films of the 1950s, using our outward similarities to infiltrate American culture and do it one better. Canadians have been ironically redefining the very essence of the American media for decades. Take, for example, the codifying guru of them all, Marshall McLuhan.

So why not rejoice at the fact that I am permanently and legally below the forty-ninth parallel? Moreover, I am *extraordinary,* for goodness' sake, if only for my thumbs. Put me on national television and let me espouse gun control and socialized medicine! Let's put the "u" back in colour before anyone notices!

My friend Jim used to get weepy whenever the customs workers at Kennedy would say, "Welcome home, Mr. Woods." He was grooving on the theatrics of nationality. I understand that. There was a Kodak commercial in which a young Asian American girl, presumably a war orphan, now a valedictorian, thanks her white adoptive parents. I cried shamelessly whenever it came on. I was moved by that myth of belonging, of being from somewhere. And, I suppose, of then being from somewhere else.

On my first trip back to Canada after getting the card, the official at the airport fed it through the small computer at her desk. My identity whirred out of the slot on the other side.

"I also have my Canadian passport, if you'd like to see it," I said.

"That won't be necessary," she said.

Necessary or not, at that moment I would have liked nothing more than for her to have said to me, as I had been raised to say, "Oh, yes, please, Mr. Rakoff."

THE BEST MEDICINE

If anybody's responsible for my being on this flight, it's that damn Preston Sturges, who started it all in his classic film, *Sullivan's Travels,* when he had Joel McCrea say, "There's a lot to be said for making people laugh. Did you know that's all some people have? It isn't much, but it's better than nothing in this cockeyed caravan." Sullivan, a successful movie director of comedies tired of his own lightweight artistry, yearns to make a grand, Odets-like homage to the workingman, working title *O Brother Where Art Thou?* In his zeal for hardscrabble first-hand knowledge and street cred, he takes to the open road of Depression-era America along with the sublime Veronica Lake—she of the peekaboo hair and diner coffee voice. Sullivan gets what he's looking for as his good luck dissipates almost immediately. Separated from Lake, taken for dead by his friends back in Hollywood, he ends up on a chain gang in the bayou. One evening, when the prisoners are given the treat of attending movie night in the local one-room church, Sullivan sits in manacles and watches as the men around him are transformed and transported by a Mickey Mouse cartoon. He comes to realize the importance of his chosen genre.

Sullivan's now canonical epiphany has been taken up as the battle cry of the comedy industry. Clownliness is next to godliness! And so I am bound for Colorado and five days of laughter, laughter, laughter, at the Sixth Annual U.S. Comedy Arts Festival.

I have not rented a headset, but even silent, the predicament being mutely acted out on the in-seat TV screen is one I cannot fail to recognize. Three women stand around an hors d'oeuvres table at a wedding. The Cute One with Kooky Hair is ranting, presumably about marriage as an outdated ritual for which she has no time. We already know that she doth protest too much, which will prove quite funny when she later falls head over heels in love with the fellow she now professes to loathe. Her diatribe is adorable, her antic ringlets bounce and fly about like the springs of a cartoon clock gone kerflooey. The bride arrives and throws her arms out in greeting. The Short One—and, therefore, the least attractive and consequently the one with the best lines—moves forward with her own arms outstretched as the bride runs right past her. Chagrin! (Grin.) All of it, the frozen stances indicating pauses for laughs, the cadence of line-line-joke, line-line-joke, the facial expressions, all serve to construct a narrative all-too-easily gleaned. Dialogue would almost seem like overkill.

Certainly dialogue would interrupt my reading, because at the same time I am plowing through Freud's *Jokes and Their Relation to the Unconscious* as fast as I can. This is my vain attempt to attain some erudition about the nature of funny in the few hours remaining before my arrival in Aspen. Somewhere over Iowa, I read that jokes, like dreams, can serve as releases of anxiety or as a palatable means of transmitting unsuitable impulses, like hostility. Or smut, which Freud says is "directed to a particular person by whom one is sexually ex-

cited and who, on hearing it, is expected to become aware of
the speaker's excitement and as a result to become sexually ex-
cited in turn."

Theory becomes practice at thirty-three thousand feet
when, not forty minutes later, the man in front of me asks the
very attractive woman beside him if she has seen *American Pie.*

"What? You think I can't get myself off?" she responds in
kind, quoting back to him a line from the movie about a girl
who masturbates herself with her flute.

The meaning and mechanics of humor have been on my
mind the last few weeks, not for the least reason that I've been
fielding calls from the festival's corporate sponsors. Initially I
thought I had won a lottery for which I hadn't even bought a
ticket, given the jubilation of the woman's voice on my answering machine. "Hi!" she cheers, her voice impossibly happy
and upbeat, her high spirits having relieved her of the need to
breathe between words. "I'm calling for Listerine PocketPaks,
and we really hope you'll report on our 'Clean Up Your
Mouth' Award, given to a comic at the festival not just for his
or her talent, but for their clean mouth approach to comedy!
See you in Aspen!"

Hers was not the first such call. She was beaten to it by a
pert young thing from American Eagle sportswear—official
outfitter of the Aspen comedy festival. They will be taking
celebrities "shopping," which means giving them free clothing
in exchange for "some style-related quips." She, too, hopes I'll
want to write something about it. The festival's publicists have
given out the phone numbers of all the journalists attending.

Actually, I'm not really here as a legitimate journalist (what
else is new?). I'm here because I've been here before. I attended the very first USCAF in 1995 as a performer (or "artist,"
as my laminated ID badge said), acting in a play written by my
friend David. In its maiden year, it was a somewhat smaller and
woollier affair, still redolent with the fantasy of the Young
Upstart loaded with gumption, plucked from obscurity, flown

to the Rockies, where he wows the network brass and walks away less than a week later with an HBO special or a sitcom deal.

This was not our dream, since not one of us in the play had overwhelming television aspirations. In fact, I remember us as feeling fairly miserable and out of place in Aspen, a fact that was confirmed for me when I ran into a producer I had met five years previously. "What are *you* doing *here?*" she asked, looking at me as if I were a ghost.

Where once the USCAF was the Sundance of struggling comics, now it has become, well, the Sundance of struggling comics. The whippersnappers already arrive with deals intact, like One-Hit Wonder, for instance, a disconcertingly milk-fed group of seven Oklahomans in their early twenties. The tale of their career trajectory as told in the festival program is a romantic one: it all started when the boys were discovered in Austin and set up with an industry showcase where "they met and fell in love with several CAA agents."

Now, disencumbered of the rude mechanics of the starmaker machinery, the festival can concern itself with its cultural mission: to elevate comedy to a state of grace it has never known before. It's an exhausting whirl of five days of films, stand-up, performance, and tributes to various stars of comedy, like director Barry Levinson and icon *de la République* Jerry Lewis.

It's not that the desire to be taken seriously is an unfamiliar or inappropriate impulse, even among comedians. After all, nobody wants to be told they don't matter, even as they play a rendition of "The Star Spangled Banner" in armpit farts. But the question remains of how, or even whether, to honor in one place something that comprises not only the likes of Groucho Marx and Jacques Tati, but also the spit take and the banana peel slip, not to mention the unleashing upon an innocent and unsuspecting public of a Pauly Shore or a Gallagher. It's a fairly broad field, a bit like having a festival in celebration of perspective in painting. Yet such are the noble goals of the Comedy Arts Festival. The "Arts" says it all, or would very much like to.

The USCAF is the bastard love child of Sturges's epiphany. This is the comedy industry's attempt to battle its own inferiority complex, to confirm and ratify the cultural importance and nobility of clowning, and to not just elevate it on par with its more sober cousin, drama, but take it one step further and ratchet it to the status of moral virtue.

And what better place to serve as the Olympus for all this high-minded cavorting than Aspen? Almost anywhere else, as it turns out. With its population of nine thousand swelling to upward of seventy-five thousand at peak season, Aspen is very beautiful, let no one tell you otherwise. Sitting in a bowl of majestic mountains, the air is positively minty with coniferous freshness. The snow, which falls softly and almost constantly, blankets everything in a dazzling, magical whiteness. But as is the case with most enclaves that exist solely for the pleasure of the rich, Aspen is ridiculous. Like a weakly chromosomed Hapsburg or an ornamental dog bred through generations to conform to a tortured and rarefied aesthetic, what has resulted is something of a skittish and monstrous character: indolent, useless, and mean-spirited. Shop after shop sells moose antler chandeliers, armoires resembling rustic mountain cabins, and sundry other bits of faux frontier chic. In Aspen, if you want to buy a framed Dubonnet poster from the 1920s, a T-shirt that reads "Warning: I have gas and I know how to use it," or washable silk skiwear with a Navajo blanket pattern rendered in sequins on the back, you're in luck. If, on the other hand, you find yourself with a staph infection and in need of a pharmacy, I'm afraid I have some bad news.

Moreover, it seems a decidedly strange choice to stage a festival devoted to an art form that requires lung capacity—either for the telling of jokes or for the cardiovascular exigencies of the pratfall—in a place with a decidedly thin atmosphere.

When I acted here, I promptly lost my voice and had to resort to breathing from an oxygen tank before the performance.

To its credit, the USCAF is no free-for-all. Much of what I end up seeing over the next five days ranges from the very funny to the inspired. But even this gives rise to another central tenet, attendant to the Comedy Is Good myth: Comedy Is Hard. Certainly well-rendered comedy is hard. All things done well require practice and work. But for most funny people, being funny is as inevitable as being double-jointed; it is a worldview formed long before words. One is born funny. The adage, as is, is incomplete. It should be Comedy is hard . . . if you're not funny. Pirouettes are almost impossible . . . without legs. Jokes can be honed, made better, tighter, and cleaner, and people can even be made funnier. But you can't really make someone funny who isn't.

This is not as awful as it sounds. It's not an etched-in-stone dichotomy, for starters; everyone has their moments. But more important, if being funny is not a moral virtue, as the USCAF would have us believe, then neither is being unfunny a moral failing.

This brings up yet another, far more important misconception: that being comically generative and having a sense of humor are one and the same thing. The former is among the least important things in the world, while the latter is among the most. One is a handy social tool, the other an integral component of human survival. It bears repeating a third time: Not being funny doesn't make you a bad person. Not having a sense of humor does.

A digression: I haven't been forthcoming about two things so far. The first is the why, the nut of this story, the underlying reason I have been sent to Aspen. All stories are assigned and embarked on with a secret agenda. The one given to me (another lie! the one I wholeheartedly posited to my editor of my own accord) was this: I have come to Aspen to flay Robin Williams—who is to be the subject of a tribute here. I have been entrusted with the task of exposing the rainbow-suspendered-Patch-Adams-Jakob-the-Liar-Twinkling-Elf as the personification of everything that is wrong and normative and middlebrow in our culture: the walking representation of the USCAF's taking itself too seriously. I have come here as a hatchet man. By week's end, my stated target will have proved less deserving of attack than I had hoped, alas.

My other obfuscation is a personal one. Where I purport to care not one jot for a life of treading the boards, that my presence here as a reporter is role and reward enough, that I have no lingering yearning to perform, I am not entirely telling the truth. I walk around with a touch of the broken impotence of the octogenarian at the college stadium, both dreading and yearning for someone to ask him about the final moments of the big game of '37. When a woman does come up to me in line at an event and not only remembers my performance from five years before, but asks me why on earth I've given it up, as if giving it up had been a choice of mine, I want to die of shame. "I'm a writer now," I tell her, my voice upbeat, making a can-we-get-the-check scribbling motion with my hand.

"If *The Vagina Monologues* takes all my audience, I will be really pissed," comedian Marc Maron worries aloud. He has come to do his one-man show, *Jerusalem Syndrome:* an exegesis of his life, including stints in Hollywood, where he subsisted on "sleep deprivation and cocaine" ("I began to feel like I had clairvoyant powers and that unseen psychic tendrils were emanating from my head and I could feel the souls of buildings and read the minds of people coming towards me; I began to feel like I was working for some unseen mystical force and I was assigned Hollywood to understand the evil that resided there"), and a trip to Israel with his wife and an exploration of the prophet-like fervor, Jerusalem syndrome, that afflicts so many pilgrims to the Holy Land.

Maron is blazingly smart, rapid-fire, and very funny, and his show is a brilliant and relentless screed. It begins with a photograph of a ten-year-old Maron against a science-fiction background of deep space. The voice-over is the disembodied female voice of benign and meaningless authority. The kind of voice that usually tells you to try your call again or fasten your seat belt, "Ladies and Gentlemen, *Jerusalem Syndrome* is brought to you by . . ." and thus unfurls a long litany of the factors of Maron's existence and character, including "a faulty diaphragm, Eastern Europe, Crest, Similac, Boston University class of '85, and bacon."

There was a time when comics like him were less of a mainstream rarity. By today's standards he is a little dark, a little highbrow: in a word, "downtown." Memories of an age when a Maron could be a prime-time star come flooding back at the Smothers Brothers tribute. All the major tributes take place in the Red Brick Community Center auditorium. Perhaps the discomfort of the plastic folding chairs has been contrived as a means of reinforcing the flesh-mortifying seriousness of learning and academic rigor of these important evenings. The floor is sodden from everyone's wet boots, there is no room for coats, and the prime center aisle of seats has been reserved for industry people.

Bill Maher moderates a discussion with Tom and Dick and three of the writers from their show, Steve Martin, Mason Williams, and the offputtingly loquacious and combative Bob Einstein (a.k.a. Super Dave Osborne, a.k.a. the real-life brother of Albert Brooks).

It's a fractious and gemütlich reunion. The brothers and
their writers talk over one another, finish each other's sen-
tences, bicker, and reminisce in the noisy manner of people
who have known each other forever. During a brief and rare
moment of silence, the preternaturally mild Dick says almost
mournfully, "This is just like a lot of forums I see on television,
that nobody ever finishes a thought." Everyone in the audience laughs at this unwitting slam of Maher's own show,
Politically Incorrect, which is more often than not a cacopho-
nous free-for-all screaming match between celebrity dunder-
heads.

Even in real life, it seems, straight man Dick Smothers
doesn't get the good lines. It's quite clear that Tom, despite
his having played the dim brother, was the driving force behind the act as well as the television show. Whatever talk there
is of the risks taken, censors faced down, writers protected,
and so on, it is always spoken of as having been by Tom's
agency. Even the years seem to have been kinder to Tom. It
might just be a healthy après-ski glow, but Tom, always a
pleasant enough looking fellow, has become in his late middle
age what can only be described as beautiful. His skin has been
burnished, his bone structure tuned up by a team of German
engineers, accented at the corners of his eyes and sides of his
mouth with a tracery of fine golden pleats.

Dick looks fine.

The years fall away from both of them when the lights go
down and the footage of *The Smothers Brothers Comedy Hour*
starts to play. I'm a sucker for funny agitprop, and it's hard
not to get nostalgic watching clips of the boys in their twenties
take on race, drugs, Vietnam, and censorship with such un-
self-conscious temerity. It still seems fairly groundbreaking
and risky even by today's supposedly wiser, hipper standards.
Tom, officiating a wedding between a black man and a white
woman, pronounces them man and wife and then, looking off

camera, says, "The rope, please." A montage of the late Pat
Paulsen's repeated presidential bids, played poker straight,
shows him getting off the campaign plane in different states,
professing to feel as if he's finally home while maligning the
state from which he's just come. It could be news footage from
the recent election. This was all so subversive back in 1969 that
the boys were fired from their own show by no less a power
than Richard Nixon via Bill Paley. Tom laments the near total
lack of prime-time political satire on television today. There is
the collective regret up on stage that television is no longer a
medium for ideas. "It's not even a medium for entertainment,"
adds moderator Bill Maher in an insight bizarrely lacking in
self-awareness. "It's an advertising medium that inadvertently
presents some entertainment once in a while." This isn't entirely true, thankfully. For clever political satire, we still have
Jon Stewart, possibly the great wit of his generation.

Stewart aside, however, Smothers and Maher are largely
correct. Where the more gimlet-eyed humor of the past was
meant to galvanize us to action, comedy in these more solipsis-
tic times is designed as therapy. Laughter, we are told, is good
for us, a means of social redress. Behold Sturges's monsters.
As Sturges described it, humor was a kind of noble salve to our
national malaise. But this is a very different America from that
of *Sullivan's Travels,* when the widespread destitution of the
Depression was still fresh in the minds of a nation at war. One
wonders what exactly the national malaise might be in this, the
longest economic boom in history. If anything, it's a personal
and baronial one, like gout. In our extreme comfort, laughter
is something we use not to escape circumstance, but to create
circumstance, something to wake us up out of our privileged
torpor, to make us feel we've done something good just by
showing up. Think no further (if you can remotely stomach it)
than Roberto Benigni and his Holocaust romp, *Life Is
Beautiful,* the most loathsome example of a belief in the cura-

tive powers of levity: his recasting as fable the chilling effi-
ciency of the Nazi killing machine; his rendering of a death
camp as a budget resort low on blankets; but above all the vile
disrespect evidenced by the film's equation that those who
perished were, I suppose, just not funny enough to turn those
frowns upside down and survive. . . . Well, I just can't say
enough bad things about him. Even his buffoonish appearance
at the Academy Awards, where he didn't even have the de-
cency to throw a bone to the millions who died in order to give
him such great material by calling for that shameless yet requisite moment of silence: a vile, vile, morally reprehensible,
shitty film! One wonders how Benigni might make some of the
twentieth century's other geopolitical tragedies more palatable: *A Fish Called Rwanda; The Stop-It-You're-Killing-Me Fields; To
Serb with Love,* perhaps?

It's not as if we haven't given our beloved comedy stars precisely such license. Those who take on the comic-as-social-
worker mantle seem to do so only after achieving a certain
amount of acclaim. It is an affliction that strikes the overly
adored and hyperaccoladed. Much like you-know-who. Four
days and counting until his gala evening.

In the meantime, for Benigni-esque messianism, admittedly on a smaller scale, there is always Dan Castellaneta's ex-
ecrable one-man show, *Where Did Vincent Van Gogh?* I go in a
fan; Homer Simpson is a character of complete genius with
which any actor could justify an entire life's work. I am not
alone, either; this is an audience of Castellaneta fans, including *Simpsons* creator Matt Groening. As with most audiences
when there is a live celebrity on stage, our laughter is performative, disproportionate, and noncontextual: a semaphoric
ass kiss across the footlights. Here we are, famous person! We
get you!

Where Did Vincent Van Gogh? is an ethereal and sanctimo-
nious snooze involving an alien, played by Castellaneta, sent

on a Diogenes-like quest to find seven noble characters, each of whom he morphs into by fritzing and popping like a television changing channels. We've seen them all before: the snotty waiter, the gay drag performer, the Indian cabdriver, a bit as a ventriloquist's dummy meditating on who's actually the dummy and who's controlling who (get it?), Sister Wendy Beckett as a randy nun desperate for ravishing defrockment at the painted hands of a naked Tintoretto saint, and so on. In an Icarus-like moment of hubris, Castellaneta says, "I don't do characters, they do me." Wrong both times.

The nebulous, New Age-y notion of the show is that all these sterling souls are being gathered to restore our faith in some unnamed thing (presumably not one-person theater). It's a bad sign when I start counting the unused props on stage. Only two wigs, one stool, an easel, and a dropcloth to go. I begin to pray to an unfeeling God to please make Castellaneta multitask. The damnably overdue conclusion, a we-are-all-one-and-you-are-me-and-I-am-the-alien bit of jetsam, is vacuity dressed up as depth. If I were sixteen and stoned, my world would be rocked. (Ecstatically, I am no longer either.) Castellaneta takes his curtain call with the earnest face and noble purpose of one who has been called to Teach.

Still, he is Homer Simpson, and stardom will out. "It's just so great to be able to be made to laugh again," says a woman outside the theater, her hand against her chest. Her voice is suffused with the relief of a patient whose fever has just broken or whose boil has been lanced.

I roll my eyes in "get her" disgust at an acquaintance I met my first time here. "Weren't *you* thinking of doing a one-man show?" he says to me.

"Oh, no. I'm a writer now," I protest, hammering my index fingers up and down in make-believe hunt-and-peck.

Trying to lance my own boil of rancor, I decide to go with

the Aspen flow by swimming in the outdoor superheated lap pool at my hotel. It snows huge flakes, the accumulation of which has greatly improved the dun-colored mountain dotted with celebrity megahomes facing me. Now, turning white, I begin to understand a little bit better the attraction of such a place as this. But there is no oxygen here, and after four laps I am wheezing like a midcoital Nelson Rockefeller. Fed up with the salubrious "Smell that air!" heartiness of the place, I opt instead for taking up smoking again, having kicked my two-pack-a-day habit some eight years previously.

Better even than tobacco, however, is that evening's tribute to Nichols and May. Mike Nichols, while largely unchanged, was always a bit soft, but Elaine May remains the beauty she was, looking startlingly good and trim in cigarette pants and a tight silver-white shirt. They are greeted with thunderous applause when Steve Martin introduces them at the Red Brick. May's microphone isn't working, and Nichols and Martin look on in amusement as a young technician comes out and fumbles with her chest. Looking up at him, sloe-eyed and mock nervous, she says, her voice vaguely suggestive, "I don't know who you are, but . . ."

Like the Smothers Brothers evening, we are treated to clips of their classic material. Even after decades—many of the routines are older than I am—it all looks newly minted. A phone conversation between a Jewish mother and her infantilized son is the Platonic ideal of what, in other hands, has become a cultural cliché. Its nuance, interaction, and depth of character haven't been improved upon since.

Aspen is crawling with comic celebrities, but it can be safely said that Nichols and May are the only people at the festival who actually effected a paradigm shift in the culture. As charter members while at the University of Chicago of the Compass, which later became the Second City, they invented improvisational comedy. Talk about honoring perspective in painting; everyone working in comedy today is indebted to this innovation (including, almost especially, what's-his-name. T minus two days). Nichols and May are almost dismissive of their contribution, portraying themselves as nothing more than two smart-ass undergraduates, the logical product of place and time.

"The thing about the University of Chicago," says Nichols, "is that it was the most referential place I think that I've ever been in. You could say Dostoyevsky and get a big laugh."

"We started doing scenes in a bar. So everybody else in the bar was drunk and from the University of Chicago," says May, shrugging. "We just did what they did."

There's nothing false about these twin displays of modesty. The two aren't even overly invested in talking about themselves. Nichols simply up and ambushes the proceedings about halfway through the evening. Turning to us conspiratorially, he produces a copy of a speech given by Martin some weeks prior at the American Comedy Awards in Los Angeles, which he proceeds to read aloud, while May kills herself laughing and Martin curls in on himself, a thrilled and embarrassed cocktail shrimp.

"When I was told I had won this award, I spent the next three weeks trying to, well, care. As I look into the audience, I see familiar faces. Some unfamiliar. . . . Many I may meet and then forget that I met. . . . Some I will not meet, think I have, and say, 'Haven't we met?' Some of you are wearing lacy white cotton panties. Some of you are in boxer shorts. But we're here because of a common love: me."

It is brilliant vintage Martin, with its skewering of self-importance and oh-little-me unctuousness. Its underlying indictment of awards shows and self-complacent festivals like the

USCAF itself is largely lost on the audience. Wresting control
of the evening once more, Martin asks Nichols to explain what
he meant when he said, many years previously, "A laugh is like
an orgasm."

Nichols is not entirely sure. "I think I may have meant
that, like an orgasm, a laugh has no politics," he says. "You
know we're all being beaten to death with correctness, so I'm
obsessed with correctness and the harm it's done." This last
statement garners spontaneous applause. "I don't know . . .
I'm not talking about cruelty . . . because that's not funny.
But if something is really funny, then it's sort of cleansed itself.
. . . If it seems funny to you, then by and large, it's okay."

I bridle a bit at this professed standard of objectivity because, fan though I may be, Nichols directed and May wrote
The Birdcage, a retrograde, hateful, and archaic film in which, it
must be said, both the laughs and the orgasms have politics. It
is that mutual exclusivity Nichols posits between funny and
cruel—that if something is funny, then it necessarily follows
that it becomes intrinsically good—that just doesn't hold water for me. Vitriol does not reflexively turn to nectar when it's
funny. If that were true, everyone would win the clean mouth
award, heaven help us. Didn't Nichols see *South Park?* Proof
that a funny, cruel joke can stay beautifully and brilliantly
both.

What seems to distinguish a lot of the cruelty of today—
from the Farrelly Brothers to the egalitarian humiliations of
American Pie—is its winking acknowledgment of the politics it
is flouting. Nowhere is this veneer of knowing recuperation
more apparent than when Adam Carolla and Jimmy Kimmel,
co-hosts of *The Man Show,* take the stage at the festival's
Advertising Age magazine award for the funniest commercial of
1999. Carolla and Kimmel are the It Boys of the postpolitical.
Their program with its beer-and-babes aesthetic has made
loutishness hip once again, only this time for a generation

barely into its twenties. The demographic in the room is decidedly young and evenly divided among men and women. I have landed in MTV's Winter Break. I can feel my ever more visible scalp prickling with age.

"Are those goddamn 10-10-220 people here?" asks Carolla. "Dennis Miller wants his credibility back." The audience reacts with a mock-scared "whoah," thrilled to finally smell blood in the water. Carolla's dis clearly isn't merely about the fact that the Dennis Miller spots are wincingly unfunny, nor is it because a colleague has sullied himself by making commercials—*The Man Show* boys make spots for beer and 1-800-COLLECT themselves, after all. The difference between them and Miller comes down to the fact that Miller posits himself as a humorous Cassandra, exposing the lies at the very heart of our society. Carolla and Kimmel don't purport to stand for anything but having a good time.

The commercials are very funny, and the winner, a spot for Ameritrade, is hilarious. But they are, simply stated, commercials. There was a time when there would be something a little eggheady about watching compilations like this. One was either in the advertising biz or at the very least a weekend McLuhanite; either way, you had to go to some lecture hall or broadcasting museum to see them. In this epoch where science continues to assiduously study Center Square Whoopi Goldberg to see if there is a product she will not endorse, there is no sense here in the audience that the medium might have something to do with the message. That at the end of the day, something is being sold. But who am I to argue with the sheer joy and paroxysms of delight of the people around me as they laugh at all of this dot comedy? They might as well be a chain gang watching a Mickey Mouse cartoon.

Hours later I chance upon the Antero Room at the St. Regis—American Eagle HQ. Looking inside, I see none other than Dick Smothers, sitting in a director's chair, earnestly talking to a rapt audience of three sportswear publicists about when he bought his first piece of microfiber. The remaining shards of my illusions are ground down into dust.

At least I witnessed this only on the last day of the festival, the evening of which will finally lead me to my prey and the closing-night gala, the American Film Institute tribute to Robin Williams. It is the festival's most prized ticket and very hard to get. In the press room the transcribers are worrying aloud how they will ever be able to write down the torrent of words that will invariably pour out of Williams. He is spoken of in the awed, reverent, and vaguely terrified tones usually reserved for an approaching hurricane. As mere mortals, we are powerless in the path of the Williams juggernaut. He is considered a priori brilliant, and the task of simply keeping up would be task enough, even if he weren't so funny!

I have yet to meet anyone outside of the press room, however, who does not actively revile Robin Williams. "Can't people see through that shit?" asks one comic rhetorically when the subject comes up. The evening is set up as a one-on-one interview between Williams and Monty Python alumnus Eric Idle. It will presumably involve a serious discussion of Williams's film work, but there is the widespread and chuckling expectation that Williams can be trusted to riff with his usual frenetic abandon. I am aghast to find that the stage has been set up with shelves of props, dwarfing Castellaneta's modest selection of dramatic aids. Tonight we will observe, it is assumed slack jawed with amazement, the catalyzing of comic jewel after comic jewel to be hurled forth for our wonderment and delectation.

AFI director and CEO Jean Picker Firstenberg opens the floodgates of smarm as she kicks off the evening: "Comedy is cherished by those of us who love movies, and I believe it is vital to the national well-being. But all of us know that funny movies are . . . often snubbed by the cultural intelligentsia. The time has come for funny films to have the last laugh."

It strikes me that with Mike Myers, Jim Carrey, and Adam

Sandler commanding $20 million a movie, funny films are already having the last laugh, and quite a few of the laughs prior to the last laugh. Moreover, I don't know of a single film studies intellectual who wouldn't rank the work of Buster Keaton on par with that of Ingmar Bergman. So what precisely is Picker Firstenberg talking about? It is in that phrase *vital to the national well-being.* Is the lack of an Oscar nomination for, say, *Big Daddy* really a miscarriage of justice, a wound to the Republic on par with the suppression of the Pentagon Papers? And while she may well have been given a limited time to speak, it seems ridiculous that the head of the American Film Institute cannot come up with a broader continuum of cinematic comedians than Chaplin, Keaton, Lloyd, and "the man we are here to honor tonight." She talks about Williams as if he were penicillin or the polio vaccine: "You have made this world a better place. Regardless of the delivery system, your creative impulses are uncontainable."

Once again the clips begin, interspersed with footage of Williams's stand-up over the years. Watching his live act over almost two decades—the endless reel of cocaine jokes and spoofs of Valley-speak—drives home two little-acknowledged facts: First, Robin Williams is a really good, competent actor when he shuts up, which is never. And this is too bad because, second, Robin Williams isn't actually all that funny. He is the Billy Joel of comedy, accessibly catchy in the initial moment, but with the shelf life of yogurt.

From the moment the interview begins, Williams is off. There is the theory among some psychologists that spontaneity is really nothing more than overlearned skill. Certainly Williams's rapid-fire delivery and shifts of accent attest to this. The tropes and shamanistic visitations feel tinny. The feng shui consultant (a trend, it must be said, already a few creaky years past) who minces around the stage expounding on energy flow and open space is precisely what we have come to expect from him; ditto generic Black Guy. A pirate's tri-corner hat becomes his means of accessing the seafaring persona of his own penis, "Har har har!"; picking up a photo-graph of Al Gore, he utters the predictable "Please don't listen to my speeches and operate heavy machinery"; George W. Bush's alleged drug use is trotted out. It feels warmed over and dated even as the words leave his mouth. Never has spon-taneity seemed so practiced, the very opposite of fresh. The overtested child who knows all too well that the mirror is really an observation window.

To his credit—and the detriment of my evil purposes—Williams comes off fairly well and keeps his dewy-eyed Angel of Laughter in check. Surprisingly, the evening's allotment of treacle comes from Eric Idle, who opines, "They are the finest people in the world, aren't they, comedians?" Yes, not like those pushy, conceited Doctors Without Borders, and don't get me started on that bitch Daw Aung San Suu Kyi. He then follows it up with the self-aggrandizing, "It's not a normal thing to do, is it, to be funny?" Even the disingenuous Idle must know that being funny, or at least the attempt thereof, is arguably the most normal human impulse there is (aside, per-haps, from our need for the quick and convenient fresh breath provided by Listerine PocketPaks!).

I had arrived here thinking of that oft told urban myth of the man who, newly diagnosed with cancer, checks himself into a hotel room for the weekend with videotapes of his favorite funny movies, only to emerge days later with the carcinoma beaten into remission by a flood of levity-induced endorphins. There's really no arguing with Preston Sturges. It does seem wholly preferable to try to weather the vicissitudes of this cockeyed caravan through levity rather than through tears, but it bears repeating that even though laughter may well be "the best medicine," it is not, in point of fact, actual medicine. One needs more than laughter to round out and sustain life.

On my last morning I eat a ridiculously extravagant breakfast of salted pork products and eggs, washed down with a gallon each of coffee and orange juice. Not the smartest meal to have before boarding the notoriously bumpy ride to Denver, affectionately referred to by locals as "the vomit comet." But I do not care; I am entering the hypomanic state born of the prospect of my imminent departure. I emerge from the hotel to smoke my last cigarette only to find the sky gray with the ominous promise of flight-canceling snow, lowering down onto the surrounding mountains like the lid slowly closing on a lobster pot.

I'm suddenly reminded of that legendary medieval torture wherein infidels and malefactors, their chests constricted by tight leather straps, have salt poured on their feet. Goats are then brought in to lick the salt off and the victims expire in horrible, suffocating guffaws, unable to escape or draw their next breath.

I panic at the prospect of being trapped in this chic mountain enclave, awaiting the thaw. I see the icy months before me, still trying desperately to clamber up on stage, trapped in the audience in a circle of leather-tanned ski bunnies, listening to ceaseless routines, our throats ragged and the skin of our faces chapped and cracking open from the never-ending laughter.

CHRISTMAS FREUD

I am the Ghost of Christmas Subconscious. I am the anti-Santa. I am Christmas Freud. People tell me what they wish for. I tell them the ways their wishes are unhealthy or wished for in error.

I will be sitting in a chair, impersonating Sigmund Freud in the window of Barney's department store at Madison Avenue and 61st Street every Saturday and Sunday from late November until Christmas 1996. My Freud imitation is limited to growing my winter goatee, being outfitted in the store's tweediest, most 1930s merch, and sitting—either writing or reading the *New York Times* or *The Interpretation of Dreams*. I did not have to audition for the role. I got the gig because I am friends with the store's creative director. At the same time, I don't suspect that he was inundated with applicants.

My window is a mock-up of Freud's study, with the requisite chair and couch. It is also equipped with a motorized track on which a videocamera-wielding baby carriage travels back and forth, a slide projector, a large revolving black-and-white spiral, two hanging torsos, and about ten video monitors that play Freud-related text and images: trains entering tunnels, archetypal mothers, title cards that read "I DREAMED I WAS FLYING" "I DREAMED MY TEETH FELL OUT," and so on. The other Barney's windows this Christmas season are devoted to Frank Sinatra, Martin Luther King Jr., the Beat poets, and Blondes of the 20th Century. The Freud window, titled "Neurotic Yule," is the only live one.

When I sit in the chair for the first time, I am horrified at the humiliation of this, and I have no idea how I'm going to get through four weekends sitting here on display. This role raises unprecedented performance questions for me. For starters, should I act as though I had no idea there were people outside my window? I opt for covering my embarrassment with a kind of Olympian humorlessness. If they want twinkles, that's Santa's department.

I am gnawed at by two fears: one, that I'm being upstaged by Linda Evans's wig in the Blondes window next door; and two, that a car—a taxi, most likely—will suddenly lose control, come barreling through my window, and kill me. An ignoble end, to be sure. A life given in the service of retail.

Sometimes for no clear reason, entire crowds make the collective decision not to breach a respectful six-foot distance from the window. Other times they crowd in, attempting to read what I'm writing over my shoulder. I thank God for my illegible scrawl.

Easily half the people do not have any idea who I'm supposed to be. They wave, as if Freud were Garfield. Others snap photos. The waves are the kind of tiny juvenile hand crunches one gives to something either impossibly young and tiny or adorably fluffy. "Oh, look, it's Freud. Isn't he just the cutest thing you ever saw? Awww, I just want to bundle him up and take him home!"

There are also the folks who are more concerned with

whether or not I'm real—this I find particularly laughable, since where on earth would they make mannequins that look so Jewish?

My friend David wrote down what people were saying outside:

"Hey, he really looks like him, only younger."

"Wait a sec. That's a real guy."

"He just turned the page. Is he allowed to do that?"

"Who is that, Professor Higgins?"

If psychoanalysis was late-nineteenth-century secular Judaism's way of constructing spiritual meaning in a post-religious world, and retail is the late twentieth century's way of constructing meaning in a postreligious world, what does it mean that I'm impersonating the father of psychoanalysis in a store window to commemorate a religious holiday?

In the window, I fantasize about starting an entire Christmas Freud movement. Christmas *Freuden* everywhere, providing grown-ups and children alike with the greatest gift of all: insight. In department stores across America, people leave display window couches, snifflingly and meaningfully whispering, "Thank you, Christmas Freud," shaking his hand fervently, their holiday angst, if not dispelled, at least brought into starker relief. Christmas Freud on the cover of *Cigar Aficionado* magazine; Christmas Freud appearing on *Friends;* people grumbling that here it is not even Thanksgiving and already stores are running ads with Christmas Freud's visage asking the question "What do women want . . . for Christmas?"

If it caught on, all the stores would have to compete.

Bergdorf Goodman would leap into action with a C. G. Jung window—a near perfect simulation of a bear cave—while the Melanie Klein window at Niketown would have them lined up six deep, and neighborhood groups would object to the saliva and constant bell ringing in Baby Gap's B. F. Skinner window.

There is an unspeakably handsome man outside the window right now, writing something down. I hope it is his phone number. How do I indicate to the woman in the fur coat, in benevolent Christmas Freud fashion, of course, to get the hell out of the way? Then again, how does one cruise someone through a department store window? Should I press my own number up against the glass, like some polar bear in the zoo holding up a sign reading "Help, I'm being held prisoner!"?

   I come up to the store for a photo-op for a news story about the holiday windows of New York. It is my thirty-second birthday. I am paired with a little girl named Alexandra. By strange coincidence, it's her birthday as well. She is turning ten. She is strikingly beautiful and appears in the Howard Stern movie. She is to be my Dora for the photographers. (Alice Liddell to my Lewis Carroll is more like it, she is so dewily alluring.)

   In true psychoanalytic fashion, I make her lie down and face away from me. I explain to her a little bit about Freud, and we play a word association game. I say, "Center," she responds, "Of attention." I ask her her dreams and aspirations for this, the coming eleventh year of her life. Without pausing, she responds, "To make another feature and to have my role on *Another World* continue." She sells every word she says to me, smiling with both sets of teeth, her gemlike eyes glittering. She might as well be saying, "Crunchy!" the entire time. But she is lovely. I experience extreme countertransference.

I read a bit from *The Interpretation of Dreams* to her.

"Is this boring?" I ask.

"Oh no, it's relaxing. I've been working since five o'clock this morning. Keep going."

Even though her eyes are closed, she senses the light from the news cameras outside. She curls toward it like a plant and clutches her dolly in a startlingly unchildlike manner. The glass of the window fairly fogs up.

I've decided to start seeing patients. I'm simply not man enough to sit exposed in a window doing nothing; it's too humiliating and too boring. My patients are all people I know. Perhaps it is because the patient faces away from both the street and myself that the sessions are strangely intimate and genuine. But it's more than that. The window is, surprisingly enough, very cozy. More like a children's hideaway than a fishbowl. Patients seem to relax immediately upon lying down.

S. begins the session laughing at the artifice and ends it crying on the sofa talking about an extramarital affair. Christmas Freud is prepared and hands her a handkerchief.

K. has near crippling tendinitis and wears huge padded orthopedic boots. The people watching think it's a fashion statement. She wears a dress from Loehmann's, but I treat her anyway.

H., a journalist, likes to talk with children and write about them. Perhaps that is why his shirt is irregularly buttoned.

I. is not happy in his relationship. His boyfriend stands outside among the watchers in the gray drizzle, his face a mask of dejection. It's quite clear he knows exactly what we are talking about, although he cannot hear a thing we're saying.

In fact, the real transgression, in this age of tell-all television, is not that the therapy, no matter how sham, would be conducted in a store window. It is that its particulars remain private and confidential.

I'm told that a woman outside the window wondered aloud if I was an actual therapist. I suppose there must be one in this town who would jeopardize his or her credibility in that way. *I've scheduled our next session for the window at Barney's, I hope that's okay. . . . Huh . . . you seem really resistant. Do you want to talk about it?*

A journalist is doing a story on the windows for the *Times*. He asks me if this is a dream come true. "Well, it is a dream. It's logical," I reply. "One of my parents is a psychiatrist, and the other is a department store window." He doesn't laugh at my joke, but it's half-true. One of my parents is a psychiatrist, and the other is an M.D. who also does psychotherapy. I've been in therapy myself for many, many years. The difference between seeing a shrink and being a shrink is not only less pronounced than I imagined it might be, it feels intoxicating. When my own therapist says to me, "I have a fantasy of coming by the window and being treated by you," I think, Of course you do. I feel finally and blissfully triumphant.

When I sit there with a patient on my couch, my pipe in my mouth, listening, it feels so . . . perfect. Like any psychiatrist's kid, I know enough from growing up, and from my own years on the couch, to ask open-ended questions, to let the silences play themselves out or not, to say gently, "Our time is up," after forty-five minutes. The performance feels real, the conclusion of an equation years in the making. And more than that: it is different from being in a play. The words I speak are my own.

The press coverage for this escapade is extensive and

strange. There is such desperation for any departure from the usual holiday drivel they have to churn out, the media come flocking. Yet the public doesn't particularly want to read about Christmas in the first place. It's like trying to jazz up a meal nobody wanted to eat anyway. People from newspapers and television are asking me these deep questions about the holiday, the nature of alienation at this time of year, the sub-textual meaning of gifts, things like that, as though I actually *were* Freud. In a moment of odious pretension that is extreme even for me, I can hear myself actually saying the word *Durkheim* to the fellow from Dutch television. A stringer for a London paper arrives late for his interview—his third wife gave birth to his first child the night before. When Marlene Dietrich's rendition of "Falling in Love Again" comes up on the repeating tape loop that plays in the Blondes window next door, he stops midsentence, and says, "Oh, this is the song I always sing when I start to have an affair." It's a disconcerting moment for me, not only for his inappropriate disclosure, but also because with very little effort, I could be drunk with the power of my Freudness and advise this stranger on his serial infidelity problem.

I get a call from the store that Allen Ginsberg might be persuaded to stand in the Beats window on Sunday and, if he wants to, would I speak with him? "I have no sway over Mr. Ginsberg, but if he has something he'd like to talk about, I'm certainly available," I reply. Not entirely true—I'm pretty well booked.

The whole Allen Ginsberg thing depresses me a bit, though. Then again, if he can see it as some cosmic joke, why can't I? I feel indignant and very territorial. Impostors only! No real ones in the window! Fortunately, it's moot; he doesn't show. When he dies the very next year, I am relieved all over again that he didn't succumb.

A street fair outside seems to have brought a decidedly scarier type of spectator. They are a crowd at a carnival sideshow and I the Dog-Faced Boy. A grown woman sticks her tongue out at me. Later, during a session, a man in his fifties presses his nose up against the window, getting grease on the glass, presses his ear up to hear, and screams inaudible things.

When I leave after each stint, I put up a little glass sign that reads "Freud will be back soon." It's like a warning. The post-modern version of "Christ is coming. Repent!" "Freud will be back soon, whether you like it or not." "Freud will be back soon, stop deceiving yourselves." In the affluent downtown neighborhood in Toronto in which I was raised, someone had spray-painted on a wall, "Mao lives!" to which someone else had added, "Here?"

My window is a haven in midtown. I can sit here, unmindful of the crush in the aisles of the store, the hour badly spent over gifts thoughtlessly and desperately bought. As I sit there, I can hear the songs that play for the Blondes display. Doris Day singing "My Secret Love" and Mae West singing "My Old Flame." As I listen, I feel that they're really referring to *my* window; to Freud. Every time they come up, I find them almost unutterably poignant, with all their talk of clandestine love, erotic fixation, and painfully hidden romantic agenda.

But they might also just as easily be referring to this time of
year, with the aching sadness and loneliness that seems to im-
bue everything. Where is that perfect object, that old flame,
that secret love, that eludes us? Unfindable. Unpurchasable.

Coming up to my final weekend as Christmas Freud, I start to
feel bereft in anticipation of having to take down my shingle. I
began as a monkey on display and have wound up uncomfort-
ably caught between joking and deadly serious. A persona that
seems laughable at times, fated for me at others. I know this
will fade, but for the moment I want nothing more than to continue to sit in my chair, someone on the couch, and to ask
them, with real concern, "So tell me. How is everything?"

I'LL TAKE THE LOW ROAD

The very unshaven young priest from Italy on the train up to northern Scotland has the handsome, tormented look of a defrocked cleric from a De Sica neorealist flick. He wears the uneasy countenance of a man made to question his beliefs, having tasted the apostate joys of, say, carnal love with a beautiful widow. Or perhaps his anguished expression is the result of the egg mayonnaise sandwiches in the dining carriage. To avert just such a crisis of faith, I've brought my own *sopresatta* and cheddar on rye, much to the delight of the Seeing Eye dog who immediately goes rooting through the bag of food I have placed at my feet. "He's not nicking your lunch, then, is he?" asks the dog's owner, seated beside me. Well, he would know if his dog was nicking my lunch, because he turns out to be one of those very special blind men who can actually see. Whatever his visual impairment, it must be minimal because, no joke, he spends the entire train journey reading and writing voluminous notes on the rules of conduct for some sort of tournament. His handwriting is better than mine, so it makes me wonder if perhaps I am witnessing an Easter miracle, right here on British Rail.

It has been sixteen years since I was on a train moving northward through Britain. The last time was at age nineteen when I was on my junior year abroad in London. Sitting across from me then had been a beautiful young American with a backpack. We made pleasant if not fairly stultifying conversation. He was from the Bay Area and let me listen a bit to his Windham Hill tape, *Colors* or *Songs for the Road Within* or something. Music that, if you're not buying a futon at that very moment, is essentially aural torture. With little to talk about, the subject turned to movies, as it does. *Amadeus* had just come out in the States, and I asked him how it was. "Well, if you like Bach, you'll love it," he told me.

A dog's head is far heavier and generates a great deal more heat than you might imagine. After three hours my feet are crushed and very warm, but it seems like bad form to kick a Seeing Eye dog. Perhaps this is to be my penance for having skipped Passover in favor of coming instead to Britain to see friends. The significance of my actions still weighs upon me, however. I experience no small amount of guilt about not celebrating at least in some way a holiday that I've never been crazy about. To be sure, I've had some lovely Passovers past with family both blood and fictive, but Pesach's extreme levels of human contact, group activity, and plate clearing also make me a little claustrophobic. Me, I like Yom Kippur.

Still, I find myself in need of some spiritual succor at this holiday time, with my mind full of thoughts of visitations of plagues, of waters pulled asunder for the safe passage of a persecuted people, and an eternal code of ethics handed down in the desert. Going off in search of like-minded people who have placed their faith in the unseen, the metaphysical and intangible, I take my leave of my friends in both London and Glasgow and embark upon my journey. Humming the songs of *my* road within, I am making my way up to Loch Ness.

The medieval *Life of St. Columba* tells of how the early Christian, when traveling up Loch Ness to the Highlands to convert the heathen, comes upon a monster with a man in its jaws. Invoking the name of almighty God, Columba subdues the beast and frees the man. Taming a chimera and mastering the godless forces of nature is basic PR for the holy, like St. Patrick and the snakes. Given the harsh, rocky landscape I am riding through, it must have been a miracle only too easily swallowed by an ancient pagan populace.

Things get pretty quiet after Columba, monster sighting—wise, until about 1933, when the first road was built around the Loch. That's when all manner of eyewitness accounts and photographs (including "the surgeon's photograph," that most famous picture of the goosenecked silhouette rising out of the water) helped to make the Loch an international locus of phenomenology and, from the looks of the tourist shops in Inverness, the city immediately to the north, clearinghouse for the world's supply of green plush dinosaurs.

Inverness is storybook pretty, most especially along the road that winds along the river Ness, with its castle looming high over the water, facing a row of churches and handsome stone hotels. But I am not staying here. I am headed to a small town some thirteen miles southwest on the shores of the Loch proper. I kill the few hours before my bus ride eating a rather ancient piece of fried halibut, walking about the streets, and

wandering in and out of the many whiskey shops, kilt makers—
where I am assured that, even though my people were necro-
mancing, chicken-plucking Jews from deepest Latvia and
Lithuania, we, too, have a tartan—and shop after shop selling
countless items featuring the smiling, three-humped green
creature, seemingly all of it printed with the slogans "Och,
Aye, It's Nessie!" or "I'm a Wee Monster."

People are out in droves, enjoying a rare bit of sun. In a
pedestrian mall I chance upon a small trailer devoted to
protesting the use of poisons and inhumane traps against
birds of prey. There is a table arrayed with leaflets and peti-
tions. A man addresses the small crowd through a megaphone
even though we are standing only a few feet away. Despite the
amplification, the five very large birds of prey sit sleepy and
unmoving on their wooden perches. There is desperation to
the man's plea for understanding on behalf of these animals,
and one can immediately see why. It must be hard to drum up
sympathy for the peregrine falcon with its talons, sharp beak,
and bloodless, topaz stare. It briefly fixes its remorseless, murderous eyes upon me, and I am relieved to see that it is teth-
ered to its log.

The bus is delayed a few minutes after we board, which allows all of us seated on the right side to look over at the next
platform, where two skinny fourteen-year-olds kiss good-bye.
The boy looks to be fishing his house keys out of the girl's
throat with his tongue. Her friend waits, watching them un-
embarrassed, eating a chocolate bar all the while. The snog
takes a full two and a half minutes. Their heads part, a silver
thread of saliva still briefly joining them together. The boy
wipes it away with the back of his hand to polite applause on
board.

My destination, Drumnadrochit, is a small town of seven
hundred perched on the banks of Urquhart Bay. Drumnadrochit is Nessie Central, being home to no fewer than two mu-

seums devoted to the monster, the Official Loch Ness Exhibition Center, a.k.a. "Loch Ness 2000," and the Original Loch Ness Monster Museum. They are approximately five hundred feet apart and both closed by the time I arrive in the gathering, drizzling dusk. My hotel—aptly described in the guidebooks as "hideous"—sits between them. It is a modern, boatlike structure with sad touches of gentility, like the frilly sheer curtains on the windows of my tiny room that only partially obscure my view of the Dumpsters out back.

I take a brief constitutional up and down the shuttered main drag of the town, in the appropriately Scottish gloaming. I am much relieved to find the Nessie Shop still open. Here in Drumnadrochit, too, I will have ample opportunity to buy a kilt, tam-o'-shanter, dish towel printed with a shortbread recipe, tartan rain gear, Nessie fridge magnet, giant pencil, squishy bookmark, Nessie-emblazoned golf balls, eraser, or pair of "Och, Aye" or "Wee Monster" socks. And just in case the twenty-foot walk from my hotel proves too arduous, I can pop into the Keeper's Cottage gift shop just across the driveway, where, in addition to much of the above, I might also purchase a sack of chocolate Nessie "droppings." Ditto haggis "droppings." Candy shit from two completely implausible sources, the former fictional, the latter an inanimate foodstuff. Perhaps in reaction to all of this imaginary yet delectably edible feces, they also sell small sachets of potpourri, filled with local aromatics, attractively named "tiny lace smellies."

Taking my supper in the hotel dining room at an ungodly early hour—makes for a nice long evening, as they say—I try to glean a demographic of the other diners. Certainly no one else is traveling alone, and no one else appears to be looking to fulfill their Pesach jones by coming here. Most everyone sounds British, and they look fairly normal, if not just a little bit vacation trashy: the palette a tad brighter, the hair just a mite bigger than usual. I sincerely hope the foursome at the next table is talking about a nature TV program, because if not, one of the men's co-workers is an extremely accident-prone vacationer. She keeps on meeting up with huge reptiles and somehow always finds herself about to have her limbs snapped clean through by the extraordinary pressure in a crocodile's jaws. She has had thirteen operations. Their food comes. "Oh, mine looks scrummy!" exclaims one of the wives.

I retire to the bar, only five feet from my table, where I can smoke and, this being the Highlands, drink some of the local single malt. The bartender pours me a scant, Biafran finger of amber liquid. It is stronger than any Scotch I have ever had. It savors of masculinity: a tongue-numbing combination of wood, leather, smoke, and age; like drinking the board of directors of Standard Oil. After just a few sips I am thoroughly warmed, and I abandon the thought of walking back out into the town, now that it is dark and raining quite heavily. I climb the hideous stairs to my hideous room. The sheets on my single bed have been boiled and starched countless times. Appropriately, they crackle like bleached matzo as I lie upon them.

Maybe it's the time of year, or maybe it's the time of man, or maybe it's just the Scotch, but as I turn on the television, everything seems shot through with breathless anticipation, a fervent hope for the glorious arrival of some numinous presence. I watch a *Nightline*-style treatment of the resurrection story, reported as if it were late-breaking news with video remotes and on-camera correspondents. It is a valiant attempt at making religion hip and palatable for the information age: *Jim, I'm standing here in the Old City at the grave only recently alleged to have been vacated by Jesus, the renegade rabbi known to his small band of followers as Christ the Savior.* The camera pans down to the open grave and stays there. *Coming up: the woman who claims she is this son of God's mother,* <u>and</u>, *a virgin! Her story when we return.* I never thought I would be nostalgic for Charlton

Heston (a dangerous, horrible man who I sort of hope dies in a hail of gunfire one day), but it seems like a gross oversight that not one of the stations is broadcasting *The Ten Commandments.* Instead, changing the channel, I come upon a science-fiction movie where a veritable army of people waits motionless in the Nevada desert for Martian spaceships to arrive.

My thoughts drift outside my window, over the Dumpsters to the deep black water and the mythic creature under its rain-pebbled surface. Dropping off to sleep, I witness the evening's final bit of sacrilege as the vindictive Martians graft Sarah Jessica Parker's head onto a Chihuahua's body.

A large plastic model of what the monster "may" look like turns in a slow circle in the pond outside the Loch Ness 2000 exhibit, housed in a beautiful old stone building. The beast resembles a rather elegant, long-necked brontosaurus (which, as any eleven-year-old dinosaur-mad dweeb can pedantically tell you, is now known as an apatosaurus). Waiting for the museum to open, I stand at the pond's edge beside Lucy, a four-year-old with a blond bob, rosy cheeks, and bright blue eyes. She is a china doll in a dress of eyelet cotton and patent-leather shoes.

Before I can ask, "Where are your parents, little girl?" actually planning to say the words *little girl,* in my best benevolent, avuncular latter-day Fred MacMurray, Lucy screams, "Ah wona kehl the monstahr!" in a full-throated Glaswegian battle cry as she throws rock after rock. She has a surprisingly good arm for someone under three feet tall. The pebbles make a hollow *ping* as they ricochet off the animal. For now, it is just the two of us, and Drumnadrochit still seems a sleepy little Highland town, its vaunted tourist reputation as arguable as the monster itself. By eleven A.M. I will find the place overrun with families making their way across the asphalt between the four souvenir shops, their children's faces smeared with melted Nessie droppings, arguing over who next will carry the green stuffed animal.

Loch Ness 2000 is a sound and light show of surprisingly high quality, leading from room to room, the first of which has underwater cave walls embedded with plaster saurian skulls. We are told of the legacy of continental drift, the movement of landmasses and the vast prehistoric continent of Pangea. The long, steep-sided, flat-bottomed gully that became Loch Ness—the largest volume of fresh water in Britain, big enough to immerse the world's population three times over—was carved by a glacier.

All of the photographic evidence that exists is revealed to be either a shadow, bird, branch, boat's wake, or outright hoax, a number of them perpetrated by one man, a professional charlatan. This is the very man who created the surgeon's photograph. The eponymous physician was nothing more than a complicit stooge.

Apparently, all of this dubious evidence merely galvanized people to try to conclusively prove the existence of the monster. This quest, started just over thirty years ago, is spoken of as a kind of countercultural be-in, an alternative to protesting Nixon's secret war in Cambodia. "The youth of the sixties took a stand against conventional science!" *(One, two, three, four, we don't want your fuckin' laws of thermodynamics!)*

Through room after room, everything is succinctly, scientifically, and convincingly debunked. The sonar scanning of the floor of the Loch reveals nothing, not even enough fish to sustain such an animal, let alone two. There is no monster here. End of story. LN2K is a thoroughly entertaining, beautifully produced buzz kill. Still, for all its skepticism, the exit doors lead me straight out into the Nessie Shop.

Merely leading spectators out to a gift shop is a Reykjavíkian study in restraint compared with the situation at the Original Loch Ness Monster Museum, just up the road, where the exhibit is actually *inside* the gift shop. The carpet is a very bright plaid, all the better to offset the ear-splittingly loud bagpipe version of "Amazing Grace" that plays over the sound system. The museum itself is an area of makeshift plywood walls, enclosing a narrow hallway of bulletin boards behind glass, and a small interior room: the tiny theater where the filmed presentation will take place.

After paying my admission, I and the two other customers, a father and his teenage son, study the display. All the pictures of the monster in the world—every single one of which is displayed here—still don't account for many linear feet of wall space. For the rest, there are dull photos of the construction of canals and public water maintenance projects in the area, a section devoted to the midcentury attempt to achieve the on-water speed record on the Loch (apparently a rather famous event; the driver did not survive and his body was never found, although the twisted wreckage of the supersonic vehicle is shown). In yet another display case, I learn that Aleister Crowley, noted enthusiast of the black arts, maintained a house from 1900 to 1918 on the Loch in the hamlet of Boleskine. Jimmy Page of Led Zeppelin owns it now. In an uncharacteristic moment of skeptical sobriety, the museum allows as how this might not really speak to the water's darker powers, since "most records when played backwards sound like a Satanic chant."

In the display devoted to cryptozoology—that highly disputed field of study of strange, extinct, and mythic creatures—the Original Museum becomes a nineteenth-century Bowery arcade of curiosities, everything but the monstrous two-headed baby in brine. The wall text is carnival barker sensational, while the photos show unusual but by no means extraordinary animals: a Giant Squid, "the animal mythicized

[sic] by the Scandinavians as the Kraken." The Megamouth, the Coelocanth, the Spindlehorn, the Komodo dragon, "Champ," the legendary monster of Lake Champlain in upstate New York. There is the famous picture of the Japanese Carcase, which I've seen before, a rotting partial skeleton found by a Japanese fishing boat in 1977. It really is huge and enough to make one truly believe in the continued existence of aquatic dinosaurs among us, except for the fact that it was found to contain elastin, a substance present only in sharks. The description of Bigfoot, also known as Sasquatch and the Yeti, reads like a PSA for a persecuted minority. We are to think of them as a hapless giant race, now reduced to a tiny number owing to their lesser intelligence; a bony spur on the evolutionary continuum. "We must try to establish, and then ensure, their continued survival in a rapidly changing world."

The museum desperately needs a proofreader; there are many typos, and the text describing the Bermuda Blob—a white starfish-shaped, coffee-table-size piece of undifferentiated biomass—just takes off somewhere else in the middle: "Some propose that they are the remains of giant octopuses In November 1746, he died of fever, aged thirty-seven and was buried on a riverbank in Siberia unknown to science."

The elderly woman tending the cash register, and presumably running the projector, pokes her head in and tells us to make our way into the theater for the film presentation. What is this feeling of déjà vu? I wonder, as I sit in the tiny auditorium with its faded red velvet movie seats and general air of grime and threadbare opulence, watching a film that is nothing more than a projected videotape. It then hits me with nostalgic clarity: This could be a pre-Giuliani porn theater.

It's not an inapt parallel, actually. Just as no one truly believes that Adonis-like park rangers come upon priapic campers in need of "help," here too it's more about amusement and going with the flow than actual fact. "It's just a cracker of a story, that's all," said a local standing at the bar the previous night.

It's all in the name of fun, except perhaps here at the Original, where the film tips its hand immediately with its title: *We Believe in the Loch Ness Monster!* The narration, like the display outside, is slightly hysterical, whether speaking of the Loch's human history—"If these stones could talk, they would talk of the clang of metal sword upon shield, of blood spilt between clan and clan"—or its geological origins: "The rocks are quiet now, although echoes of that primeval rape still ring." There is something almost touching about seeing all of the same old photographs, convincingly debunked at the other museum not fifteen minutes prior, being presented here as hard evidence. But the movie's title notwithstanding, I don't get the sense that the folks here really believe in the monster, either. No one I talked to working at the hotel or the many gift shops seems to think about the creature at all.

The locals' widespread pragmatism is odder than it sounds. It's not like in Iceland, where the enchanted spots are so terribly unenchanting and the stories of people from another dimension able to inhabit solid rock so intrinsically farfetched. There have been some actual sightings here—albeit of sturgeons, otters, and large branches, but legitimately confusing facsimiles—and, given the imposing darkness and murk of the huge Loch, which fairly broadcasts mystery and concealment, I expected an entire battalion of the faithful. At the very least some of those Stonehenge-y, Wiccan, animist, pagan/druidical crazies eating vegetarian, playing zithers, and giving each other STDs after worshiping the dawn on the rocky shore. But there are none. Not surprisingly, the main believer does turn out to be someone with an intimate and ongoing relationship with the Loch. Alex Campbell, the water bailiff—a job whose very title would have me hallucinating just to pass the time—boasts eighteen sightings in the film.

I emerge into the gift shop, as seems to be the curatorial practice in Drumnadrochit. (Truthfully, it's the curatorial practice almost everywhere. One can scarcely walk five steps in the Metropolitan in New York without running into some makeshift kiosk hawking Monet coasters, Diego Rivera scarves, and those fucking Raphael cherubs!) I dispatch a number of pennies into one of those machines that flattens them into oval tokens incised with an image of Nessie. I adore these contraptions. I love the modesty of the objects they produce, the muscle of the heavy metal rollers, the whining creak of the gears as the stalwart copper is rendered liquid soft and ductile. I could stay at the penny machine all day, but there is more to see, or so I think. I follow a Japanese family out into the brilliant sunshine.

The *Nessie Hunter,* a small boat that fits about ten of us, is being guided over the waters of the Loch by the same man who drove us in the minivan down to the dock. The tour, even though an hour long, doesn't even begin to cover a significant portion of the Loch given its twenty-plus-mile length. The day is perfect and blue and, in a further nod to *The Ten Commandments,* the sky positively biblical with Maxfield Parrish clouds. The green felt hills to the west are dotted with sheep, while the piney banks to the east are cast in shadow. The land falls almost vertically into the water to a depth of several hundred feet.

We begin the ride a bit shy and with one last shred of credulity, wondering, almost hoping for the boat to be overturned as the waters roil and part like the Red Sea in the cutting wake of the beast's ridged and shining slate back. Out here on the Loch is the only time we feel that whatever creature might live here could be anything other than a cartoon Cecil, that cheerful, anthropomorphized playmate.

The thought lasts only moments, though. Even the chattering five-year-old boy has stopped scanning the surface. By the time the driver cuts the engine, we float peaceably, looking up at the steeply wooded slopes, taking each other's pictures. We could be in northern Ontario for all the lack of supernatural menace. Tourists wave at us as they clamber up and down the ruined turrets of the medieval castle that looms above us. We idle back into Urquhart Bay and clamber back into the van.

The driver points out the small webcam perched atop the chimney pot of a small cottage. It takes regular pictures of the water and broadcasts them over the Internet, twenty-four hours a day. He stops the vehicle, and we get out. Perhaps it's the central absence at the Loch, the materiality of the lack here, that makes us so still and quiet, but not one of us waves at the camera. We stand, unmoving, looking at an immobile camera recording an unchanging body of water.

It is a mystery to the Canadian backpacker and myself why we are almost unable to breathe as we sit on the low stone wall at the bus stop. We are outdoors, after all, a gentle breeze blows through the green bowl of Drumnadrochit's sun-washed glen, and still the air is thick and noxious with the stench of decay. The plague of the murdered firstborn meted out while I was cruising the Loch, perhaps? Finally I turn around and see the suburban tract-home-size pile of sheep droppings—not the chocolate kind, unfortunately—in the field behind us. O, for a tiny lace smelly!

My initial plan had been to be in Drumnadrochit for two nights, exploring the town and getting to the bottom of the bitter disputes between believer and infidel. I had no indication from either the guidebooks or my first view of the town, situated at the base of these verdant hills with its two exhibitions, that it would be so, well, entertainment bereft. But, having seen both museums, walked the town from stem to sternum not twice, but thrice—and enduring the increasingly suspicious stares of the man in the small cottage with the even smaller garden that still manages to hold a profusion of plaster of Paris gnomes, a small iron cannon, and a four-foot-tall bronze David—and already returned from my cruise, I am dismayed to find that it is only one in the afternoon on Day the First of a proposed three-day stay.

I take the bus back to Inverness. As we pass the LN2K museum, the parking lot attendant/entertainment, a man in full Highland attire of kilt and bandoliers, waves us farewell. The day closes in on typical gray skies and drizzle, and I have hours before the next train back to London.

I board yet another bus for a tour out of the city to Culloden Moor, site of the last battle fought on British soil, between the Jacobites and the Hanoverians in 1742. I am the only one on the double-decker with the driver. He is silent, so as not to interfere with the "tour guide," a cunningly timed Scottish female recording that somehow knows exactly when we are passing points of local interest. On our way out of Inverness, we stop on a bridge over the river Ness to see if the city's famous seals are making an appearance. They are not; we drive on. Farther out, by the Moray Firth, the inlet of the North Sea that boasts its very own population of bottle-nosed dolphins, the bus stops again for a photo opportunity so that we, or rather I, might take pictures of the creatures gamboling in the wind-tossed surf. But it is raining, and the dolphins, like the monster, the seals, and the tour guide, are a no-show. Besides, I have no camera. We drive on.

The battlefield itself is an inhumane, bracken-covered field, inhospitable and muddy, which makes the female guide's bright-voiced account of the carnage all the stranger. "The Hanoverians marched out to bloody battle after a light

breakfast and tots of brandy!" I decline the driver's offer to disembark and walk by myself along the sodden ruts of the moor.
We begin the drive back to town.

Talk of war now dispatched and with twenty minutes to go
before the tour's end, the disembodied guide now happily
chatters on about matters generally Scottish: how many yards
of cloth it takes to make a kilt (many, I forget exactly); repair-
ing stone farm walls; and Scottish cuisine. She says: "One way
that *I* like to prepare Scottish turnips is with a head of garlic
and half a pound of butter. You should try it." "But who *are*
you?" I want to cry out. You cannot know until it happens to
you, but there is almost nothing existentially bleaker than sitting alone on a bus in the rain with a driver who will not talk to
you and being given a cooking tip by someone who does not
exist.

Before settling in for the night in my inordinately cozy sleeper,
I retire to the dining car. I sit, smoking and drinking a stun-
ningly expensive beer across from a man who tucks in to his
plate of haggis and peas. I smile at him in greeting. He does
not know it, but this is our silent seder for two. I want to lean
over to him, dip my pinkie in his red wine, and count out the
plagues on the rim of his plate. We were slaves to Pharaoh in
Egypt.

I read my book and look out the window. This far north, the
evening outside is still cigarette smoke blue, even though it is
well past nine. We hurtle through the Highlands. I press my
face up to the glass. All I can see are a few sheep, out well past
their bedtimes, white spots in the gathering dark. As I have
now come to expect, they are not moving.

WE CALL IT AUSTRALIA

It all begins with that extraordinary opening shot. The camera impossibly placed in the alpine ether, coming in ever closer to the mountaintop to finally focus and settle on the turning figure—her arms outstretched, face beaming, overwhelmed with joy and music: the young novitiate, fräulein Maria. Coming in late to vespers, her color high, strange grasses in her gamine, slightly flyaway hair. How *do* you solve a problem like her? Send her away, carpetbag and guitar in hand. Have her tutor aristocratically unloved children, eventually tossing aside the three Rs in favor of teaching them simple harmony and vocal counterpoint. Make matching clothes out of the family curtains. Marry the Baron. Take the act on the road. Defy the Nazis. Open an inn in Vermont.

These few linear feet of film are what I think of whenever I hear the words *Austrian Teacher,* admittedly not a term I use all that often in my life, although about to become a staple of my vocabulary for the next eight months, starting on this sweltering July morning on the deserted campus of City College in Harlem at seven-thirty A.M.

New York City has the nation's largest public school system, with some 65,000 teachers serving 1.1 million students. There is a dearth of qualified math and science teachers here. Coincidentally, there is a surplus in Austria, with a years-long waiting list for positions. In what seemed like the perfect solution to both problems, the New York City Board of Education put up flyers at teachers colleges in Vienna. "If you can read this," they said in English, "have we got a job for you!" Today is the first of a projected two days of interviews of about fifty candidates for public high school teaching jobs in New York's five boroughs.

The interviews are being conducted in English via live video teleconferencing from Vienna. New York City public educators—high school superintendents, Board of Ed muck-a-mucks, and principals—have all gathered to ask the prospective teachers a series of qualifying questions.

New York's unorthodox plan to look for teachers so far afield has attracted a great deal of attention. In addition to myself, there are reporters from the major dailies and, most glamorous of all, a TV crew and reporter from ABC News in Washington. Two young men are busily sticking up a purple "City College" banner with brown packing tape for the news cameras' benefit.

Any job interview is an awkward affair. Any job interview with a panel of five interviewers even more so. Everyone is nervous on both sides of the ocean. Questions are repeated, slowed down. It makes for some halting progress and the occasional awkward moment of cultural preconception. When asked what previous knowledge they have of New York schools, for example, one woman answers that she heard "the kids were having guns and using drugs."

But for the most part, the Austrian teachers are hoping to

come to New York out of just such a sense of adventure; to experience another culture firsthand and to improve their English, although for the most part they speak quite well. One fellow openly hungers for New York's legendary multiethnic society: "I want to see the blacks. Where I am from, there is only one black people a year," he says.

"Oh," one of the African American principals whispers. "Vermont."

Three of the men, when asked why they became teachers, innocently and unabashedly answer, "Because I love children." I don't know that an American male would answer that question in that way, even if it were true.

They all seem generally competent and acceptable. But they are almost all completely stymied by the final question: "Can you tell us anything else about yourself that should make us want to select you as one of our teachers?" Answering this question is an acquired skill even for Americans; it takes at least three job interviews before one learns that maintaining unwavering eye contact and seeming hypomanically gung ho wasn't just not weird and arrogant, it was required. For the Austrians, trained in a kind of courtly European reserve, being asked to assert their own sterling qualities in full voice seems truly baffling. A trick question straight out of *Alice in Wonderland.*

The best answer comes from the undisputed star of the day, Andrea Unger. With her doctorate in genetics at age twenty-eight, perfect English, and blond movie star beauty, she has all of us, educators and reporters alike, immediately and profoundly enslaved. This being a high school world, I am hyper-attuned to adolescent paradigms on this day, and she seems to be that rarest of legendary creatures: the popular girl beloved by students and faculty alike who, in addition to being pretty *and* smart, is also nice. She is being addressed as "Dr. Unger" scarcely four minutes into her interview. The borough superintendents are mouthing, "I want her!" out of camera range. When asked her final tell-us-why-you're-the-best question, she answers, "I don't know if I'm the very best, but I will do my best. And if that's not enough, I will do much better." We would follow her into the very mouth of hell, singing songs all the while.

"See you in September," says one of the principals after she has left the room in Vienna.

The reasons why I am the perfect person for this story are also the reasons why I am the worst person for this story. As an adoptive New Yorker, I remember vividly how challenging and frequently lonely it can be to move here when one is as green as new bamboo. As a Canadian, I also understand the whole Austria-Germany conundrum and what it's like to come from a small country, seemingly culturally indistinguishable from its dominating adjacent neighbor. But these factors are part and parcel of my unhealthy investment in, more than being opened up to, being liked by the teachers. It is why I am the world's worst reporter. I am apt to try too hard to help rather than just document my subjects. It's only amplified when I look into the innocent faces of these young foreigners.

An innocence amplified by my own ignorance. If, on the one hand, I see the meadow-sweet purity of *The Sound of Music,* on the other, I'm envisioning New York's public high schools as a sinister world of metal detectors, baggy jeans, box cutters, and white flight—an underfunded, failed social exercise; the first stop in the revolving-door prison system.

I'm not the only reporter guilty of this misapprehension. Even after a school year where there seemed to be a weekly public school shoot-'em-up everywhere in the United States *but* New York, the city's reputation as a blackboard jungle is a tenacious one. It is these exact stereotypes—the guileless, defenseless foreigners being used for target practice by young toughs—that have so piqued the interest of the national media. Certainly, it is more than the clever resourcefulness on the part of the Board of Education that has gotten us up here at seven-thirty in the morning, with the temperature outside already well above eighty degrees.

It's also what gets me and thirteen other reporters and sound and camera people all the way out to Kennedy Airport one month later on an exceptionally muggy and toxic August Friday. We sit in the California Lounge at the Delta Terminal, falling in and out of conversation, and slumber as we wait for the Austrians to get through customs.

The posters on the walls are, paradoxically, of London, Paris, and Amsterdam. Perhaps the only thing that seems authentically California to me about the California Lounge is how boring it is. Some of the reporters are talking about the official statement from the teachers union: "We're pleased they're here, but it's regrettable that New York doesn't pay its teachers more." The starting salary for a teacher in New York City is just under $30,000, which sounds pretty good, and is even a living wage in New York, but it's not Easy Street by any means. We are all briefly diverted when those same two young men from City College come with that same purple banner and try to tape it up on the wall. But the California Lounge will not stand for extra adornment. The banner keeps falling down, and they finally give up.

When eventually the teachers arrive, they seem tired and hot as they sit indulgently and somewhat dazed, listening to the official greetings from the Austrian consul general and people from City College and the Board of Ed. By contrast, I am energized, my heart racing a bit, as if I were in the presence of major celebrities. This is especially true when I see Andrea Unger.

Looking at them, I remember my own seventeen-year-old self, coming to New York for college. My introduction to the city was from the safe and privileged haven of a fairly cloistered campus, under the watchful eye of a well-paid, if not actually caring, administration. As public high school teachers, the Austrians will not be similarly coddled.

Andrea and three other teachers—Lutz Holzinger, Elke Rogl, and Nikolaus Ettel—are all assigned to teach at Franklin Delano Roosevelt High School in Bensonhurst, Brooklyn. Bensonhurst was the scene of some racist violence a few years back. I am, quite frankly, terrified at the thought of going to Bensonhurst. As far as I knew, if you weren't white, Italian American, and straight, you stayed out of Bensonhurst.

It's not just a fear of inner-city New York teenagers that fuels my trepidation for them; it's teenagers in general, having been one myself. I remember the rumor and innuendo, the erroneous, slandering lives we constructed for our teachers. If any of it were to be believed, we were being taught by the most dangerous, antisocial dregs of society, a rogues' gallery of the kind of misshapen, alcoholic, sexual deviants that you wouldn't even let out into the general cell block population, let alone near a bunch of kids. I shudder when I think of what I and my cutthroat little pals could have done with the accents and strange surnames of the Austrians before me.

I can hardly keep the fear out of my voice when I speak to my Austrian Four. Andrea asks me if I've heard of FDR and whether it's a nice school. My response is a poker-faced, "I think, uhm . . . I think the FDR High School is going to be a completely interesting experience for you." *(You bought the old Lawson estate? Ain't nobody lived there since that horrible murder twenty-five years ago. If you want my advice, you'll turn around and leave this place!)*

"Whatever it means, huh?" She is somewhat less than appreciative of my candor.

Nikolaus—Nikki—is a small, finely made man in his mid-twenties. He is, in a word, adorable, which to my mind also means, in a word, a goner.

"I've heard it's a big school," he says.

"It's huge. It's four thousand kids," I say in a voice strangulated with panic.

"Four thousand?"

"I just found that out."

Nikki attempts to maintain composure. "Okay. Really huge, and so I expect that it might be somehow anonymous. We will work it out very easily, I hope, and I'm glad I can come here."

I've also found out that FDR's four thousand kids are from seventy-two different countries representing thirty-two different language groups. One-third of them are identified as limited-English-speaking youngsters, meaning they've entered the United States within the last two or three years. Easily 60 percent of the entire student body was born outside the United States. This ethnic diversity is a bit of a surprise. Not exactly the bastion of xenophobic thuggery I'd envisioned. The Austrians will be right at home.

Still, I come by my alarmism honestly. I have learned this custom over the years as I have settled into being a true New Yorker. This is how we welcome foreigners to our shores. Because we are so often frightened by living here, we are annoyed and offended when visitors fail to show the proper signs of terror. So we try to scare the living daylights out of them.

There are those who would say that my fear is an outdated remnant of a pre—Gilded Age New York, and perhaps it is. With the city now being overrun with packs of ravening Internet millionaires, it sometimes seems like the most frightening thing for many New Yorkers is getting to Citarella before they sell the last piece of sushi-grade tuna. Where once we scared people with oblique auguries of physical peril and tales of the ignored screams of a Kitty Genovese, we now resort to frightening strangers by talking about housing.

"So do you have a place to live yet?" I ask Nikki.

"We have a dorm for a week, and I have to look for an apartment. I want to live together with some Brooklyn teachers because of low cost."

Unmollified by his positive attitude, I continue. "Yeah, it's a particularly expensive time in New York City. Rents are kind of . . . well, you never know. I'll see you." Mission accomplished for now, I move through the crowd of new arrivals to do more damage.

Luckily enough for the Austrian teachers, their introduction to life in New York City and its public school system will not be left up to the paranoid, hysterical likes of me. They will, instead, sit through a series of days of orientation sessions at City College, where they will be turned into fully functional residents, with Social Security numbers. They will see Miss Licorice—her actual name!—the representative from the Chase Manhattan Bank, about opening accounts. They will be taught how to write checks and, worst of all, look for apartments.

That seminal Feet of Clay realization in childhood when it dawned upon you that your teachers go to the bathroom is as nothing compared to watching respected pedagogues trying to find an affordable rental apartment in New York City during a Wall Street boom, no laughing matter . . . well, if it's a laughing matter, it's in that bitter, rueful kind of way.

I want to help and befriend them. In an effort to distance myself from the ubiquitous media, I have, on this day, another scorcher, donned a pair of too-short cutoffs and Birkenstocks. I give the Austrian Four my card and urge them to call me—a friendly, half-naked stranger. Not surprisingly, I do not hear from them. Moreover, against seemingly insurmountable odds, after one weekend of hitting the streets, they all have homes.

The elephant that is New York City brings out the proprietary blind man in most New Yorkers, each fiercely advocating his separate version. It has turned all of us into Stalinists of one sort or another. I get deeply worried, for example, when the sunny, retrograde, Giuliani-loving, retail-worshiping version of New York threatens to overtake all others. I still maintain that the city can be a lot tougher than the daisy-strewn Gotham of the loathsome *You've Got Mail,* and I hold fast to the idea that the teachers will find that out in short order.

But if I and the rest of the media are nervously anticipating the Austrians' bloody defeat upon the urban battleground of inner-city schools (like the cameraman who, upon hearing that they will be teaching high school, whistles, asking no one in particular, "Anybody know karate?"). Then the educators who actually work in the New York public school system are laboring under their own set of preconceptions.

We are at the Board of Education in Brooklyn, where the Austrians are being introduced to working in public education. They are seen as buttoned up and humorless, a stereotype I roundly reject after spending the better part of fifteen minutes reading (and copying down) the back of the T-shirt of the cut-up sitting in front of me, an exhaustive, comparative religion thematic variation on the truism "Shit happens." It is a fifteen-item list, including "Zen: What is the sound of shit happening?", "Judaism: Why does this shit always happen to me?", and "Jehovah's Witness: *knock knock,* shit happens."

They are further told that in the New World teachers use modern teaching methods, unlike, it is implied, Austria. The New York educators—only a few of whom have ever been in an

Austrian classroom—warn them time and again about the dangers of the dreaded "chalk and talk," that driest, most outmoded Teutonic kind of pedagogy, where one stands at the board and lectures, with no room for inquiry or discussion.

One of the more useful moments in the whole orientation, however, comes not from educators, but from a group of actual New York City high school kids who have come to meet them. The students give them a quick lesson in New York Slang. They pass out handwritten flash cards: Bounce, You Played Yourself, Whatever's Clever, Flavas, the Bomb, Phat, You Buggin'. Andrea is asked to use one of the new terms. "I think you all look very jiggy," she says to the students. They applaud.

The lesson in slang continues just a few days later in a weekly class about life in the city that is being called "New York 101" by the media. Although no one out of the media seems to have another name for it. They just call it "What the media are calling 'New York 101.' " The professor, a retired English scholar and native Brooklynite, spends the opening twenty minutes of the first class quizzing them on their various subway routes up to City College and telling them quicker alternatives. It is one of New Yorkers' favorite pastimes, telling one another the best subway routes to get someplace. As the only other resident in the room, I am thoroughly entertained and cannot resist weighing in at one point about the long underground transfer between the 4/5 and the 2/3 at Fulton Street. The Austrians stare blankly and seem exhausted.

Then comes a new set of colloquialisms, in the form of a handout. This glossary of New York argot has words and phrases like "eighty-six," "schmear," "bimbo," "maven," "What am I, chopped liver?," and "Schlepping all over town looking for some chotchkes." All of which would be very useful if it were 1949, if you were a hard-boiled cutie-pie gun moll, in the USO, a private dick, anyone from a Damon Runyon story, or auditioning for *Seinfeld*. There is even an entry for "a quick pop," meaning an alcoholic drink, a term probably not in use since the prime of Cab Calloway.

What becomes evident over the course of the orientation is that the Austrians are also being given an unvarnished glimpse, albeit an unwitting one, into what it can truly be like to be a student in public high school in North America: hours spent sitting, listening to lecture after lecture, frequently droning, and frequently about things they will never need to know—the bureaucratic structure of the Board of Education, for example, or how to say, "Eighty-six the whiskey down wit' da schmear."

It turns out I'm not all that up-to-date myself. When Lutz and Andrea ask me if I know where they should go dancing (after I tamp down my initial excitement, mistakenly thinking they have asked me to go with them), I can come up with the names of only two places: Limelight, closed for over a year at that point; and Palladium, a block from my apartment. When I get home that evening, I will see that it, too, isn't just no longer open, it has been torn down.

I try to be of help in other ways. In exchange for two carpets that I'm not using, I get Lutz and Nikki to agree to show me their apartment—huge and sunny in the Sunset Park section of Brooklyn—and take me along with them when they go to see their school for the first time, a few days before the beginning of the semester. The media attention surrounding them shows no signs of abating. Their schools are fielding inquiries from CBS, Austrian TV, and a Japanese television crew. They tell me how fed up they are getting with being portrayed as being too scared to take the subway, unfamiliar with different ethnicities, and oblivious to social problems. Lutz gently points out that the small matter of the genocidal civil war in former Yugoslavia is happening not too far from Vienna. There are refugees coming into Austria every day.

Lutz and Nikki are not men who are unaware of the outside world. "We are international people," says Nikki, whose girlfriend is spending the year working in Moscow. I ask them if they have drugs and teenage pregnancy in Vienna. Lutz replies, Of course, although not to the extent of New York City, obviously. But it's really an idiotic question. Where do I think they come from: Shangri-La?

Franklin Delano Roosevelt High School is beside a huge cemetery. Literally beside the graveyard, with headstones coming right up to the building, like a teen exploitation film joke—a summer camp actually built across the lake from an insane asylum. Architecturally, the school is one of those early sixties structures of glass and cinder block. It is quite an attractive building, actually, and there's a friendliness, a sense of community, about the place; it's in perfect repair, the floors gleam.

We run into the school guidance counselors. "We saw you on the news!" They treat the Austrian Four like celebrities. Andrea is still a little surprised by all the scrutiny and occasionally frustrated by some of the questions:

"People keep asking us where we are from. We tell them Austria, they say, 'Oh, Australia.' And we say, 'Austria,' and they say, 'Oh, but we call it Australia.' I tell them, 'No, it's absolutely different,' and they say, 'Oh, but it's the same area.' "

At almost that exact moment, a passing security guard asks excitedly if they are the Australian teachers.

Despite the fact that she has two days to get the school ready for four thousand students, and that Andrea, Lutz, Nikki, and Elke are by no means the only new teachers starting this year, FDR's principal, Adele Vocel, takes the time to sit down with them in the conference room. She doesn't talk to them as though they are Austrian teachers, just teachers. And it's not for my benefit, either. I am, in a word, tolerated. I follow along as Lutz and Andrea are shown the newly renovated science labs, given the ninth-grade biology curriculum, and introduced to some of their fellow teachers. Like everyone we meet at the school, they project this sense of shared purpose and excitement; they make it look like great fun, and there's no false nobility here, either; there's none of that sun-washed earnestness of films like *Dead Poets Society*. All of it goes a long way toward dispelling my fear (I mean, of course, *their* fear) of the school year that begins in two days' time.

The New York these Austrians will be working in is very different from the New York inhabited by the members of the media covering them. For starters there's a lack of irony to almost everyone I encounter. Nobody is making constant air quotes or dropping their voices in "what, me serious?" disaffection. No one acts as if they've seen it all before. At one point at the Board of Ed during a teacher orientation, Adele Vocel reads a poem called "Average" to a room full of adults. It is a work of cudgel-like subtlety, telling of a student who, having been told he is average, loses the volition to pursue his dreams:

> 'Cause since I've found I'm average
> I'm just smart enough to see,
> It means I'm nothing special
> That I should expect to be.

Later on, at a reception at the Austrian consulate, another woman in public education plants herself in the middle of the room, takes a laminated card from her pocket, and intones an extended affirmation to the effect of "One hundred years from now, it will not matter how much money I made, what kind of car I drove, how big my house was, whether or not I was famous. WHAT WILL MATTER is that I made a difference in the life of a child!" Her delivery is almost one of umbrage.

Generally, the words *I'm just going to read you this poem* elicit feelings of mild embarrassment in me: how avid, how earnest. I admit that I was a little amused when I first heard these two poems. Neither of them is very good poetry, after all. But on reflection, I realize that they achieve precisely what poetry is meant to accomplish: they edify, they elevate, they speak to an underlying truth not immediately apparent, they change the way one looks at things. I had thought the Austrians were heading off into a quagmire of cynicism, institutional neglect, and violence, when, in fact, they were entering a world I hadn't imagined—a world where being earnest and avid and passionate is anything but embarrassing. The embattled tone of the woman with the laminated poem is completely justified. In a society fixated precisely on how much money one makes, what kind of car one drives, how big one's house is, and whether or not one is famous, the education of young people isn't just undervalued and underpaid work. It is looked upon with a sense of benign dismissal. Precisely the weary, slightly ashamed indulgence of a beloved, albeit overpoliticized, relative in the habit of intoning bad poetry in the middle of one's elegant cocktail receptions.

It's been made clear to me that I am not welcome in the classrooms once the students arrive. FDR's obligation is to the kids, and I would be an unnecessary distraction. I see the sense in this, so I invite the Austrian Four for dinner instead. And they accept and seem happy to be asked.

Although school has been in session for at least a month, they have been teaching for only ten days, owing to the Jewish holidays, in which they have become rapidly versed. The whole experience still feels new and strange and surreal to them. "If I woke up now at home, I would say, 'Oh, that's a crazy dream,' " says Elke.

I observe as how the reality of their situation seems to lie somewhere between an urban war zone and Maria von Trapp. "Maria von Trapp?" they ask me. They have no idea who I am talking about. I find myself explaining *The Sound of Music* to them.

"No Austrian has ever seen *The Sound of Music*," Andrea says.

"You should teach us to sing 'Edelweiss,' " Nikki suggests. They have each been asked more than once if it's the Austrian national anthem. When I ask them what they know of Julie Andrews (Julie Andrews, for God's sake!), Andrea replies, "*Mary Poppins.* And *Victor/Victoria.*"

The dinner is jovial and comfortable. I feel that they now know me well enough that I can ask them what has been on my mind since that first day in the California Lounge at JFK. I ask them, finally, about Jews: whether they know any, if there are any in the program. The closest contact to those few remaining in Austria, it seems, is that Nikki taught in a kindergarten near Vienna's Jewish quarter and saw some.

"My grandmother doesn't like them," Elke says matter-of-factly.

I suppose I'm glad she feels such ease in my home, but I'm a little put off by the complete lack of contrition or guilt by association in her tone. As the child of immigrants who rejected apartheid and left South Africa in 1961, decades before it was politically expedient or fashionable, I still never failed to explain and apologize for *my* grandmother's presence in Cape Town when she was alive.

That one moment aside, the dinner establishes something between us. We become friendly. I get fairly regular calls from the Austrian Four, questions about excursions they should take, where might they find Indian food, and so on. In late November I take them to see one of the city's great and most overlooked landmarks: the New York Panorama at the Queens Museum in Flushing Meadow. It is an enormous diorama of the five boroughs, with scale models of every single building in the greater metropolitan area. I checked. Everything is there, right down to a half-inch replica of the four-story brownstone where I live. Spectators walk around its perimeter on a catwalk above.

The videotaped presentation about the display's construction that plays constantly on a loop begins with an announcer exclaiming over a Gershwin score, "New York City! The Big Apple! Making it big! The Arts Capital of the World!" This bit of cheap New York, New York propagandist metaphor, seems a little naive. Because what one actually sees when looking at this accurate depiction of the city in its entirety is that most of the city—the New York that is New York to most New Yorkers—is actually the Bronx, Queens, Brooklyn, and Staten Island, which all contain some pretty vast areas of urban blight and desolation.

We stand over the Brighton Beach and Rockaways part of the diorama, Manhattan far behind us. And while it's certainly the most crowded of the islands and its buildings are the tallest, it is also noticeably the smallest. Seeing it from here, from the equivalent of a few thousand feet up, Manhattan's disproportionate influence, the power of its few over the millions in the outer boroughs, seems not just strange, it seems feudal.

All this time I have been wondering how the Austrians would deal, expecting them to crumple when actually faced with real New York, with the smug assurance that a boroughist Manhattanite like myself knows what real New York is. But more than almost anyone I know, these four teachers have been thrust into an environment where most everyone is from somewhere else. Even in my search for an authentic backdrop to this particular interview, I brought them to a large simulacrum, when probably the most authentically New York place is the block they live on.

Night descends upon the miniature city—their city. The

sky darkens and black lights illuminate the buildings, whose windows seem lit up in millions of pinpoints. A few moments later it is morning again, and another day dawns on the greatest metropolis on earth. The orchestra on the video plays. It is all one can do not to stretch out one's arms and turn around like some singing nun on a mountainside for the sheer joy and beauty and hugeness of it all.

Tiny planes on invisible wires come in for landings and take off from the diorama airports. And far higher than all of them, an airplane sails through the sky, tracing its path from across the Atlantic westward to somewhere else on the continent.

Nikki wonders aloud how any plane passing over New York could possibly resist landing here. Indeed, how *could* any aircraft ignore the very center of the universe? Spoken like a true New Yorker.

BACK TO THE GARDEN

It is difficult nigh on impossible to construct either my Figure-Four or my Paiute deadfall trap, to say nothing of having them work, in the dark, in the rain, at eleven P.M., after a seventeen-hour day of lectures and demonstrations during which I have already been instructed in (among other things) the sacred order of survival—shelter, water, fire, food; how to make rope and cordage from plant and animal fibers; how to start a fire using a bow drill; finding suitable materials for tinder (making sure to avoid the very fluffy and flammable mouse nest, as it contains hantavirus); the signs of progressive dehydration; how to find water; how to make a crude filter out of a matted nest of grass; how to distinguish between the common, water-rich grapevine and the very similar yet very poisonous Canadian moonseed; how to make a solar still with a hole covered with a sheet of plastic (and how to continue the condensation process by peeing around the hole); and the Apache tradition of honoring those things one hunts, be they animal, vegetable, or mineral. All of this in the scarcely day and a half since arriving at the Standard class of Tom Brown's Tracking, Nature, and Wilderness Survival School.

The Standard is the first of twenty-eight classes offered by the school. A Wilderness 101 of sorts: a week-long, lecture-heavy, intensive introduction to outdoor primitive skills and nature awareness. Skills and awareness at the very heart of the bildungsroman that is the oft told life story of Tom Brown Jr.

Briefly, it is as follows: Growing up in the Pine Barrens of New Jersey in the late 1950s, a young Tom spends almost every waking moment from the ages of seven to eighteen in the woods under the tutelage of his best friend Rick's grandfather Stalking Wolf, a Southern Lipan Apache. Brown's apprentice-ship ended in 1968 upon his graduation from high school. He spent the next ten years working odd jobs to make the money necessary to spend his summers testing his skills in unfamiliar environments across the country—the Grand Tetons, Dakota Badlands, Death Valley, and the Grand Canyon—living in de-bris huts and scout pits of his own devising and subsisting on food he foraged or killed himself, often without even a knife. (Brown was 4-F owing to a chip of obsidian that had lodged in his eye years before. Stalking Wolf had predicted years earlier that "the black rock" would keep him out of Vietnam.) After a decade Brown reemerged into society with the single-minded mission to teach others and lead them back to the woods and a love of nature.

All of this is told in *The Tracker*, Brown's first book. It is a tale of an adventurous boyhood of limitless self-reliance, in an unfathomably Arcadian wilderness. It makes for com-pelling, if not always entirely credible, reading: part Richard Haliburton, part Carlos Castaneda, part *Kung Fu*. Grand-father, already an octogenarian in 1957 when Tom first meets him, is a man of almost Buddha-like wisdom with a penchant for posing oblique, seemingly insoluble riddles with premises along the lines of "Do you know how to live as the squirrels do?" and laughing discreetly behind his hand as the boys fumble for answers. The Pine Barrens themselves are portrayed as an idyll under constant threat from encroaching industry, suburban sprawl, and an advancing world with decreasing patience for the nonlinear philosophizing of an old man.

It might not be Thoreau, but it is the key to the legend that Tom Brown may very well one day become and certainly already is here at the Tracker School. At the very least, Brown is a cult figure of international stature: the best-selling author of sixteen books, Brown has trained navy SEALs in high-speed invisible survival and has helped national and state law enforcement in tracking persons, both missing and criminal (with the perplexing exception of the prosecution in the O. J. Simpson murder trial, who declined his offer of help). He solved his six hundredth case on his twenty-seventh birthday. Nowadays the bulk of Brown's tracking of humans is of the armchair variety. Having trained thousands of people who have passed through the school, Brown now has an international network of former and current students to call upon when he gets requests to track.

Many of us here for the Standard—some ninety people from the United States and Canada, four from Italy, and a young woman all the way from Japan—are aspirants, yearning to join those ranks of expert trackers. Certainly everyone is an acolyte of one sort or another. There is no one unacquainted with Stalking Wolf. Most have read at least part of Brown's oeuvre, be it one of the meat-and-potatoes field guides to wilderness survival, wild edible and medicinal plants, and so on, or perhaps one of the more spiritually oriented titles such as *The Vision, The Quest, The Journey,* and *Grandfather.*

As a group, we are almost equally divided between the sexes, and we run the gamut from the ethereal to the pragmatic—from the unbelievably sweet eighteen-year-old vegan boy from Portland to the gun enthusiast who greets me throughout the week by saying, "Hey, New York!" He brought his own food, hermetically sealed decommissioned military MREs ("Bought 'em on eBay for ten cents on the dollar after the whole Y2K thing didn't pan out. Best au gratin potatoes I ever ate"). There is the congenial soi-disant "hillbilly from West Virginia" in his fifties, and the twentysomething physics major looking to drop out for a while. For the most part, the people are friendly, intelligent, and environmentally and socially committed. I meet more than a few involved in education, in particular working with troubled teens in the wilderness. And, I am relieved to see, in keeping with the Tracker philosophy of forging an unmediated relationship with nature, they are refreshingly immune to the pornography of gear. They radiate good health as they unpack bags of gorp, apples, whole-wheat pitas, and huge water bottles. I have also come prepared with a deli-size Poland Spring, assorted candy bars, and four packs of Marlboro Lights purchased in nearby Easton, Pennsylvania, at Puff Discount Wholesale Cigarettes. (While smoking is permitted, the school is dry, with a no-drugs policy.)

I arrive on April 30, a beautifully sunny, albeit very windy, Sunday afternoon. We spend the first few hours battling the strong breeze to pitch our tents, the placement of which is overseen by Indigo, one of the eight or so volunteers, alumni of previous Standard classes, who help out for the week. Indigo hovers anywhere between fifty and seventy years old. With her sun-burnished face, craggy features, and rather extreme take-charge demeanor, she is straight out of *My Ántonia*. But she is not unfriendly, even as she tells one of the Italians, his tent staked down and ready, "Uh-uh, mister. You gotta move it about four inches that way. We're making a lane right here." She gesticulates like an urban planner dreaming of a freeway. Indigo is the Robert Moses of Tent City.

We are not actually in the Pine Barrens, sacrosanct locus of Brown's childhood. The Standard class is held on the Tracker farm in Asbury, New Jersey, near the Pennsylvania border (not to be confused with Asbury Park, sacrosanct locus of that other South Jersey legend—and Tom Brown contemporary—Bruce Springsteen). The Barrens, while apparently magnificent, also very much live up to their name. The farm at Asbury is better for teaching novices owing to its rich biodiversity. Its landscape of fields, meadows, light forest, and the Musconetcong River, which flows a few hundred yards away, offers ample flora and fauna for this week of instruction. Aside from the barn where the (hours upon hours of) lectures take place, the farm consists of little more than Tom Brown's house, a dozen or so Porta-Johns, a few wooden stalls serving as showers, and a toolshed with an awning under which sits a row of chuck wagon gas rings—our cafeteria. All activity is centered around the central yard, a scant acre-size area of patchy lawn that lies between our nylon sleeping quarters and the barn. In the center of this is the all-important fire, which burns day and night, heating a large square iron tank with a tap, where we get hot water for our bucket showers.

The instructors, whom we meet the first evening, are possibly the most organically appealing group of people I've ever encountered. They are all affable, all pedagogically gifted—there isn't a dud public speaker in the bunch—and all chasteningly competent at the endless variety of primitive skills we will learn. Like some crack team of movie commandos, they can almost be differentiated by their specific areas of expertise: Kevin Reeve, forty-four, director of the school, a John Goodman type who opted for early retirement from Apple nine years ago after taking his Standard class, paterfamilias; Joe Lau, thirty-one, resident flint knapper—his stone tools are things of beauty—ranked second in *ninjutsu* in the state of New Jersey; Mark Tollefson, thirty-two, plant expert, wild edible savant, also in charge of food; Tom McElroy as the Kid—at twenty-three years old, youth personified, a thatch-haired Tom Sawyer, possessed of a sniper's aim with the throwing stick; and Ruth Ann Colby Martin, twenty-six, resident beauty, who, it seems, can do literally everything. Polymathically dexterous, capable, strong, and funny. Joni Mitchell as Valkyrie. Even though she has earlier that day run the twenty-six-mile Sandy Hook marathon, she fairly glows. As an avowed homosexual, I generally make it a practice to seek out the amorous embraces of men over those of women, yet my heart belongs to Ruth Ann Colby Martin.

That first evening, the entire class gathers in the barn for our initial orientation session, where we are advised of the school's general guidelines and given our first taste of the ethos of the place, summed up by Kevin pointing to a sign above the stage. It reads "No Sniveling." "This is a survival school, not a pampering school," he tells us. As if on cue to prove the rustic authenticity of the place, the bat that lives in the barn swoops around our heads. We are reminded to hydrate regularly and properly, to be vigilant about the poison ivy that grows rampant on the farm. "And if you are taking any sort of medication to regulate your moods," Joe tells us, "we request that you *stay on that medication while you're here.*"

All of the instructors chime in, in unison, their voices weary with hard-won experience, "We wouldn't say it if it wasn't important."

Finally we are warned about ticks and their dreaded Lyme disease. We are to check for the small black dots twice a day all over our bodies, particularly in those dark, warm, hairy places ticks apparently so love. A proper self-scrutiny is demonstrated by one of the (clothed) volunteers, who takes to the stage holding a small hand mirror from the shower stalls. He moves it over and around his torso and limbs like a hoochy-koochy dancer with a fan, looking into the glass all the while.

As the coup de grâce, he shows us how to check our least ac-
cessible, most potential Tick Central. Turning his back to us,
he bends over, bringing the mirror up between his legs.
"Ta-da!" he says as he holds his triumphantly abject position.
We applaud.

We meet the man himself the following morning. Tom Brown
is handsome and, at age fifty, in great shape. With his silvering
hair parted neatly on the side, trimmed mustache, and pene-
trating blue eyes, there's a little bit of Christopher Street circa
1982 about him, but he resembles nothing so much as the scary
gym teachers of my youth, men who said casually hostile and
emasculating things like "You look like a bunch of girls out
there."

I'm only half-right. Brown, while blessed with deadpan
comic timing and a Chautauqua preacher's instinct for the
performative flourish, also exhibits a disquieting and ever-
present thrumming bass note of dwindling patience. This
weird duality is an acknowledged fact. Kevin has warned us
that Brown is "part mother hen, part drill sergeant." For the
uninitiated, it can make for a fairly bizarre, emotionally dizzy-
ing ride, sometimes in the same sentence. He begins with a little flattery, praising our very presence.

"The terms *family* and *brother and sisterhood* do not fall flip-
pantly from our lips." (That's nice, we think, prematurely and
mistakenly warmed to our cores.) He continues. "Even my
parents when they call, the calls are screened. I talk to them
when I want to. But you—" He indicates us, snapping back to
sweetness. "You speak my language. When I say to one of you,
'Hey, I heard a tree call your name,' you'll know what I mean.
You're more than eight to five. I'm an alien out there," he says,
meaning society. "But not with you. You're the warriors."

The only kind of warrior I feel like is perhaps one of Washington's consumptive, freezing soldiers at Valley Forge. My first night in my small rented green nylon dwelling in Tent City was an extremely frigid one, making me wonder how I will survive a whole week on one hour of sleep a night. I am not the only one having doubts about this venture. "I didn't come for boot camp," one woman says to me. "If it continues too freezing, I'm just getting in the car and going home." Morning ablutions are completely out of the question. I point out as how the chill also militates against our checking for ticks in the shower. "And the size of the mirror is this big!" she says, holding her fingers five inches apart. "How the hell am I going to see my ass in a mirror that size?"

Happily, the Standard class is not boot camp. We are not hiked miles and miles, made to gather fire wood for hours on end, or really called upon to test our physical mettle in any appreciable way. The course is not without its arduous qualities, but its rigor is an intellectual one. The days are long, from six A.M. to past eleven at night, spent largely in lecture, with actual hands-on experience making up about 20 percent of our time. During our breaks—primarily the hour set aside for meals—we practice our skills.

The main yard outside the barn buzzes with preindustrial activity: there are people making cordage, lobbing their throwing sticks at a shooting gallery of plush toy prey—an assortment of stuffed animals perched on top of logs, their foreshortened limbs, furry bellies, permanent smiles, and cuddly expressions simply begging to be taken out by a lethal piece of spinning lumber. The top prize, the object of the most murderous and blood-hungry violence, is the purple demon himself, Barney. Other students are silently fox-walking and stalking slowly across the grass, while the majority of us are trying to start fires with our bow drills.

This last endeavor is our primary milestone, survival skill-wise. The squeak of turning spindles and the sweet smell of the smoldering cedar, occasionally followed by the applause of whatever small group might be standing nearby, is a constant. I make three attempts before success, but when it comes! The thrill of sawing the drill back and forth, watching the accumulation of the heated sawdust, now brown turning to black, the small plume of smoke that rises, the gentle coaxing of the tiny coal into fragile, orange life, the parental swaddling of that ember into a downy tinder bundle, the ardent, almost amorous gentle blowing of air into same, the increasing smoke, and the final, brilliant burst into flames in one's fingers—it simply cannot be overstated how fucking cool it is. The charge is pre-verbal and atavistic. If, as Fitzgerald writes on the last page of *The Great Gatsby,* the Dutch sailors' view of the New World was the last time in history when man must have held his breath in the presence of something commensurate with his capacity for wonder, then this overwhelming awe at having finally harnessed the power of conflagration was surely among the first.

Recapturing and maintaining that sense of wonder is at the very heart of the Tracker School philosophy, which is "to see the world through Grandfather's eyes," in a state of complete awareness, living in perfect harmony with nature, attuned to what is known in the Apache tradition as the Spirit That Moves Through All Things. This awareness will provide the key to tracking animals, both human and otherwise. "Grandfather didn't have two separate words for 'awareness' and 'tracking,' " Brown says. Tracking is Brown's claim to fame. He has helped solve hundreds of forensic cases. He is undoubtedly a master at gleaning the progress over the landscape of both humans and animals, but his description of the brief, hundred-yard walk from his house to the barn is so strange and omniscient, he calls to mind Luther and Johnny Htoo, the delusional chain-smoking twelve-year-old identical twin leaders of Burma's Karen people's insurgency movement, with their claims of invisibility and imperviousness to bullets. "There had been a fox. The hunting had not gone well. She emerged at 2:22 A.M. Her left ear twitches. Another step, now fear, and suddenly the feral cat appears, she's gone!"

We won't be able to reach this level by week's end, but apparently we will be able to "track a mouse across a gravel driveway." Just one of the many skills that will save us should we ever find ourselves in a full survival situation.

"Full survival" has nothing to do with the amassing of alarming quantities of canned food, a belief that the government is controlled by Hollywood's Jewish power elite, reality-based TV programming, home schooling, or Ted Kaczynski. Full survival means naked in the wilderness: no clothes, no tools, no matches. Full survival is both worst-case scenario and ultimate fantasy. Worst case being that the End Days have come upon us, the skies bleed red, the Four Horsemen of the Apocalypse have torn up the flower beds, and we must fend for ourselves and our loved ones. (The more prosaic version of that might be a bear eating your food or your matches getting wet.) Alternately, the ultimate fantasy is we've gotten so sick and tired of taking crap from "the man" that we just park our cars by the side of the highway and step into the woods and disappear. An oft repeated joke throughout the week is "Next Monday when you go in to work and quit your jobs . . ."

Regardless of the circumstances that catalyze our move back to a State of Nature, we will survive. And survive "lavishly." Being in the woods, we are told, will become an experience akin to being locked in the Safeway overnight. "The main danger in full survival is gaining weight," Kevin avers. Nature is a bounteous paradise for those who play by the rules. That would be nature's rules, not the government's. Since much of the nation's remaining wilderness falls under the protective jurisdiction of the National Parks Service—whose rangers don't look kindly upon the wanton building of debris huts and the killing and eating of local animal populations—much of what we learn turns out to be illegal.

Case in point: animal skinning. Even picking up roadkill apparently requires a permit. For the lecture on skinning and brain tanning, Ruth Ann comes in wearing a fringed buckskin dress of her own devising—it must be said, a fringed buckskin dress with a Peter Pan collar. She tells us the story of coming upon her first roadkill buck, while taking a much needed break from writing college papers. She is, as always, adorable, sympathetic, funny, and extraordinary in both her competence and introspection. My immediate reaction the entire week to anything Ruth Ann tells me is eagerness and a wish to try whatever it is she is proposing. When she tells us to first cut around the anus and genitals of the animal and then pull them through from inside the body cavity, I think regretfully, I wish *I* had a dead animal's anus and genitals to cut around and pull through its body cavity.

I almost get my wish. After donning a pair of rubber gloves, she leaves the barn and comes back in bearing a very dead groundhog. It has already been gutted and the fur pulled down partway. It looks like a bloody baby in a nutria car coat. It hangs from a nail by the Achilles' tendons of its hind legs. The lifeless face points down, the small clawed hands sway back and forth. Grabbing hold of the pelt, Tom McElroy—the Kid—pulls, using his entire body weight. Groundhogs have a great deal of connective tissue. There is a ripping, Velcro-like sound as the fur comes down. Tom briefly loses his grip, and the wet animal jerks once on its nail, spraying the front row with droplets of groundhog-y fluid. The bat flutters around the barn throughout.

Next comes the tanning. Amazingly, almost nothing is better at turning rawhide into supple leather than the lipids in the animal's own brain, worked into the skin like fingerpaint.

A further, beautiful economy of nature is that every single animal has just enough brains to tan its own hide.

Ruth Ann made her own wedding dress from unsmoked buckskin, as well as her husband's wedding shirt. I expected her to look rough-hewn, disinhibited, and slightly tacky—like Cher—but when she takes it out of the box and holds it up against herself, we see that it is actually lovely: soft, ivory, and beautifully constructed. My crush is official.

But there will be time for infatuation tomorrow. It is getting late, and, as happens every evening, a kind of rage starts to set in around ten forty-five when people still keep asking stupid questions. I'm desperate to get to bed, having concluded the obsessive urination during breaks that starts just after supper—safeguarding against a cold, confusing pitch-dark walk through Tent City across the yard to the Porta-Johns. A small cadre of exhausted fugitives has already disappeared, making their ways back to their tents slowly and silently, without flashlights—how I envy them.

The man beside me, apropos of nothing, raises his hand and says that there is "a story" that man started society because he was "cast out of a garden because of a sin." He doesn't attribute this anecdote, leaving it a blind item from a source we might not know. He seems nice enough but potentially dangerous.

Ruth Ann's face is a placid mask of patience as she listens. "And did this bring up those associations for you?"

"Yup."

"Cool," she says.

(By week's end the instructors are pretending not to see his raised hand. He opts for making his comments under his breath. In the wild edibles lecture, when we are told to keep our grains dry to protect them from ergot, the moldy blight that causes hallucinations, he mutters, "That was before the Dark Forces turned it into LSD."

"Oh, you don't have to call them the Dark Forces with *me*,"
I want to josh him. "You can just call them the Jews.")

Perhaps it's the country air, but I rise early the next morning
at five A.M., completely refreshed. Without making a conscious decision, I head out to the surrounding fields and
woods. There is a Tracker School tradition known as "the
Twenty-Eight Club," referring to those twenty-eight individuals who managed to approach and touch a live deer during
their Standard week. It has been at twenty-eight for six years.
In my heart I know I will be the one to make it twenty-nine.

Ruth Ann has taught us the Stalk, a walk of such slow,
silent, and fluid progress that one's movements are in perfect
accord with nature. One step of Stalking, properly executed,
should take a full minute of achingly precise placement of the
outer ball of the foot, followed by the inner ball, the heel, the
toes, and then a deliberate and bomb-squad-careful shifting of
the weight. We further have to squint our eyes and close our
mouths (the whites of both will give us away) and keep our
arms folded across our middles. "Otherwise you show the human silhouette and you'll stick out like a turd in a punch
bowl," she tells us. Key to attaining the grace and calm necessary for the Stalk is going into wide-angle vision, a relaxing of
focus that not only increases one's sensitivity to one's periphery, but has the added benefit of clearing the mind: a moving
meditation.

I am alone among the trees and the low brush, the dawn
mist diaphanous. I stand stock-still and serene as I watch the
cadmium red streak of a cardinal flying by. I think of nothing.
Even the glory I will surely taste when I touch my deer seems
far off and unimportant, mired in hierarchical, tunnel-vision
thinking. I sense the branches moving to my left before I see

them. Ah! I think. An animal approaches. Welcome, fellow
creature. Come, commune with me. My breathing shallow, my
eyes at half-mast, I wait.

My conscious mind awakens, the part of my brain where my
general terror of animals resides—my incapacity to grasp why
it is animals don't simply decide to go for the jugular. I flail in
alarm like Martha Graham, snapping twigs and kicking up debris. As I flee the woods for the relative safety of the farm, I
look back to see a small weasel emerge from the underbrush,
watch my contortions for a moment, and scamper away.

I am a tunnel visionary after all. Not at home in nature, a
fact apparent to weasel and human alike, because not one hour
later one of the female volunteers asks me over breakfast,
"Where are you from?"

"New York."

"Huh. Thought so."

"Does it show?" I ask.

"A little." She leans in conspiratorially and whispers, "The
shoes."

Apparently here at the Tracker School, just as on Monadnock, people are not featuring the black plastic boot from
Payless.

Awareness starts small. Only when we understand the many
mysteries that lie within the earth's tiniest, seemingly mundane details will we be able to track animals or people.
"Awareness is the doorway to the spirit, but survival is the
doorway to the earth. If you can't survive out there naked and
alone, then you're an alien," Brown tells us. "YOU THINK
THE EARTH IS GOING TO TALK TO SOMEONE WHO
IS NOT ONE OF HER CHILDREN?" he yells.

My guess is no. To that end, we are taken out to a meadow

overgrown with heavy grasses, garlic mustard, and wild burdock, known as Vole City for its large population of the small
rodents who make their homes there. We each lie down in this
tick heaven and examine an area no larger than a square foot,
digging down, exploring.

My classmates look very idyllic and French impressionist,
scattered about here and there, supine in the sunlight, lost in
contemplative investigation. Me, I sit up, terrified at the
prospect of finding anything, especially a vole (which, my editor will laughingly explain to me, is nothing more than a harmless field mouse, as if that mitigates anything). The instructor
shows me how to root around just underneath the grass to find
the ruts worn through the vegetation by the voles as they make
their runs. I define gingerly as I use a stick to push aside the
stalks and turn over the debris, picking out the dull sheen of a
slug here, the progress of a tiny worm there.

Warming to my task, I suddenly spy, dark, wet gray against
the fresh green of a blade of grass, the unmistakable articula-
tion of reptilian digits, a hand span no bigger than this semi-
colon; as expected, it is connected to a tiny reptilian arm,
connected to a tapered reptilian head the size of a peppercorn.
The gleaming, now dead eye catches the sunlight. My heart in
my mouth, and trying to keep the panic from my voice, I call
the instructor back over and show him. He picks up the tiny
twig with the half-eaten salamander still perched on it and
holds it some four inches from his mouth, enumerating the
various classifications of the creature: the coloring, the reticu-
lations, the patterns, the species. The instructor tries, God
bless him, to draw me into a Socratic dialogue, asking me questions about what I observed. He points to the chewed-out un-
derside of the demi-lizard. "What kind of teeth made those
cuts? Are the edges scalloped? Look at the gnaw marks. That's
a great find," he says, patting me on the back.

I show my lizard to those working near me in the field. In

turn, they show me what they have uncovered. I am kind and full of noblesse oblige as I feign interest in one woman's small mound of unidentifiable animal scat. But we both know the truth: My reptile corpse makes her find look like, well, a pile of shit. For a brief moment I am big man in Vole City.

The instructor's matter-of-fact treatment of the dead salamander, the complete lack of any "poor little guy" moral component to its demise, speaks to what makes the Tracker philosophy unique among so many naturalist communities. Unlike certain Steven Seagal—moderated Buddhist retreats and Icelandic piano-teaching, elf-spotting living rooms I could mention, there is none of that falsely benign conception of nature as friendly, inherently good, tame, and prettified. Aldous Huxley, in his essay "Wordsworth in the Tropics" assails what he calls this "Anglicanization" of nature, the cozy revisionism of a force that is intrinsically alien and inhospitable: "It is fear of the labyrinthine flux and complexity of phenomena . . . fear of the complex reality driving [us] to invent a simpler, more manageable, and, therefore, consoling fiction." There is the clear-eyed acknowledgment here that things get eaten. Ruth Ann, in telling us the story of a year lived in the Pine Barrens in a house of her own construction, says, "Whatever came into my house, I ate. Mice? We just threw 'em in the fire, burned the hair off, and ate them whole. They just taste like meat, and there's something to be said for that added crunch."

She's not being heartless; in fact, she's the very opposite. For every skill we are taught, whether it's harvesting plants, using our bow drills, skinning an animal, or gathering forest debris, the first step in our instruction is always a moment of thanksgiving for the trees, the spirit of fire, the groundhog, the water, and so on. It's a strange adjustment to have to make at first (and I am not proud to admit that there is a moment at five-thirty A.M. when I serve on cook crew, as I stand bleary-

eyed with exhaustion—having gotten to bed only some five
hours earlier owing to a late night lecture on track identification—where I think I might kill the fellow who leads us in a fifteen-minute thanksgiving that includes complimenting the
rising sun for being "just the perfect distance away from us,"
which just seems fawning and, frankly, a little late in the game
to me). But truthfully, there are worse things than acknowl-
edging a continuum and connection among all things and
staying mindful and grateful of our place therein, although it
can be a hard concept to swallow before the coffee hits the
system.

Even wide awake there are some moments of fuzzy logic in
this theory of interconnectivity. Kevin, in explaining the
Apache tradition of humbling oneself before taking another
life, of being thankful to the prey, tells us this will also result in
a willing acquiescence on the part of the hunted. "Something
that gives its life for your benefit does so with gladness if you
are humble." Isn't it pretty to think so, but ascribing complicit
suicidal motives to the rabbit who licks the Cheez Whiz from a
deadfall bait stick—no matter how self-effacingly daubed on—
seems a tad Wordsworthian to me.

But such doubts become ever fewer as the week progresses.
From about Thursday on, the home stretch of the course, spirits are high. Most of us have gotten fire, and in a brilliant bit of
Pavlovian pedagogy, the food has improved markedly immediately following the outdoor cooking demonstration. Despite
the staff's urging us not to take what we are told at face value,
to go home and prove them right or prove them wrong, we're
all pretty jazzed and itching to head out into nature. That
said, among the people I talk to there is also a growing skepticism about Brown himself. It has nothing to do with his credibility, the veracity of his life story, or even the purity of
purpose of the Tracker School. Unfortunately it's personal:
Brown's drill sergeant persona so thoroughly kicks the shit

out of his mother hen. As pleasant as he may be just after breakfast—and he frequently is: sunny, sprightly, and very funny—if he addresses us after sunset, there is a darkness in him with a potential for ire that is terrifying.

In one evening lecture Brown talks about the need for us to "take bigger pictures," to see more of the world through our wide-angle vision, attuned to the periphery and a greater depth of field, to sense things before actually seeing them. "Instead of going *click, click, click,*" he minces, "go CLICK! CLICK! CLICK!" he roars at us. A few people actually flinch. Later on, in a moment meant to chide us for the persistence of our citified tunnel vision, he tells us that he has been observing us unseen from his perch on top of the toolshed. It's a creepy and menacing moment. People seem visibly shaken as we make our way to bed. We watch our backs, scanning our surroundings for heretofore unnoticed surveillance. We cast furtive glances at one another, like children trying not to attract the hair-trigger attentions of an abusive parent. Out of earshot, one young man asks a group of us softly, "You guys ever see *Apocalypse Now?*"

Of course, there are the credulous few among us who find every word from Brown's mouth a pearl, like the art teacher who indiscriminately records every moment of the week or the woman who gives me a look of such utter disdain one day as I eat a Snickers bar, one would think I was sitting there insouciantly enjoying a human turd. As far as they are concerned, everything Brown tells them is true, but they are, kindly stated, not the tannest hides in the barnyard. They wipe away a tear when Brown tells of going back to his sacred spot in the woods years later with his son, Tom Jr., and his own father:

"Passing the old spot on the river where my dad and I used to swim, little Tommy pointed out the dead plants on the bank. 'The water's sick. We can't swim here, because up the stream they put in the municipal dump.' And my dad burst into tears because it was his fucking vote that put it in. *The last vote on the town council.*" Any teacher of freshman composition would advise toning down the Susan Hayward and cutting that last detail about the deadlocked vote, with its contrived eleventh-hour coincidence and shameless play for the reader's sympathies. There is a fair amount of jaundiced eye rolling after this particular lecture.

It's too bad that Brown the Personage has this effect on people. I think it would come as something of a surprise to him, because Brown the Person, when I interview him one-on-one, is really a very nice, intelligent guy, with an undeniably noble and admirable mission in life. I do not meet with him until the Friday afternoon before the course's conclusion the next morning. By this time, while I am ready to renounce my toxic city ways for Ruth Ann and think the rest of the instructors are marvelous, my disenchantment with Brown himself is fairly entrenched.

My trepidation is only increased when I am escorted into the kitchen of Brown's home by Kevin, who does not leave. Tom McElroy, as well, sits in a chair nearby, weaving a jute bag on a small circular loom. I turn on my tape recorder, wondering if this will be an interview with the Party official surrounded by his apparatchiks. But the gestalt of the room is actually one of hanging out, not gatekeepers monitoring my questions. They crack jokes, weigh in with opinions, engage in quiet, unrelated conversations with one another. I've essentially come to the teachers lounge.

Or is it a convocation of disciples? I ask him about the cult of personality that seems to be a definite part of the Standard class.

"Oh, I try to get rid of that real quick. I tell people right off, 'Don't thank me, thank Grandfather. I'm a poor example.' I am nobody's guru." He talks about how they have to make sure to keep "Tracker groupies"—those overenthusiastic few who try to volunteer too often—at a healthy distance. "Boy, this would be very easy to turn into a cult, big time, and I just will not allow it to happen. That's the last thing I want to happen."

Noted. Yet in almost every lecture there is the requisite prefatory story from Brown's life ("When Tom was twelve years old, Grandfather told him, 'This is the year you will provide me with meat . . .' "). The accrual of personal detail forms a gospel of sorts; anecdotes are delivered in a prescribed, hortatory, liturgical style. ("He raised his hand before Tom could speak and said, 'Silence!' And he pointed a bony finger and said, 'Grandson, when you feel the same way about a stalk of grass as you feel about the deer, then you will be truly one with nature.' Tom realized at that moment that he had been ascribing a hierarchy to nature.") Granted, the stories are told to show the wisdom of Stalking Wolf, not Tom Brown, but the reflected glory of playing Boswell to Grandfather's Johnson—a term straight out of a traveling salesman joke—is a position that clearly must have its attractions.

Attractions not callously exploited, it seems. There is no line of Tom Brown sportswear, no exhortation from Brown that I buy anything while I am there, that I Think Different. The Tracker School is not the enterprise of the career opportunist. In person, Brown is not only not power-mad—having willfully kept himself out of environmental politics, not even offering recommendations of organizations people should get involved in—he's not remotely anything resembling an asshole. He has so much less of the brusque machismo of his stage persona that he seems almost as nice as one of his instructors.

I leave the house fairly won over, wishing that I had been fitted with these rose-colored spectacles somewhat earlier in the course. I return to Tent City and walk out to the field beyond it to gaze upon the sun, now lowering in the late afternoon sky. I find one of my classmates standing in the grass in the honeyed light, enjoying a water bottle full of herbal tea. We stand there amiably and peacefully, mutually imbued with the soy milk of human kindness. He holds out the amber liquid, offering it to me, and asks, "Rum?"

Our last supper is one of our own harvesting. I am on burdock detail with another fellow. The rough brown roots are over a foot long and hold fast in the red clay of the field where we dig. All ninety of us spend an hour or so cleaning, scraping, and slicing the meal. But I have never had food so Edenic in its profusion and beauty: a salad of chickweed, violet flowers, pennycress, and wild onions; a stir fry of burdock, dandelion, nettles, and wintercress buds; dandelion flower fritters; garlic mustard pesto over whole-wheat pasta (store-bought—cut us some slack); nettle soup; and spice bush tea. We are each given a trout to gut, wrap in burdock leaves, and place in the fire. After six days here, I approach this task with a strange relish. It is quite the best fish I have ever eaten.

The meal's preparation is communal and great fun, although while chopping garlic, Indigo berates four or five of us for having let one another down. Apparently our tardiness in getting inside the barn for the lectures (tardiness not really apparent to me, frankly) has made the instructors have to cut out vital things they were planning on teaching us. Things, it is presumed, they managed to impart to other, more studious Standard classes. "You're a family, a Tracker family, and you let your brothers and sisters down." If I cared more, I might mention that my family is actually up in Canada, using flush toilets at that very moment. Why Indigo felt the need to bum our stone when we were at our most cohesive and communal will have to remain a mystery only Grandfather could have explained.

The grand finale of the Standard is a sweat lodge. I generally try to avoid pitch-dark, infernally hot enclosures unless
they're same-sex and I'm a little drunk, but now that Brown is
my new best friend, I find his preamble so avuncular and sweet
that I almost consider it. He tells us we are to enter the three-
foot-high, round, straw-covered structure in a clockwise direction, leaving the area behind him free for those among us who
suffer claustrophobia. "The minute you want to get out, just
say so and we'll open the doors. I won't love you any less." I resolve to do it until he cedes the floor to Joe, who reads us the
guidelines. When I hear "crawl in on your hands and knees," I
realize that there is not Xanax enough in the world to make me
enter the sweat lodge. The other rules include taking off all
metal jewelry that doesn't sit directly against one's skin, as it
can heat up and swing back and burn one rather dangerously,
and the final admonition: "You are absolutely forbidden to
pass wind in the sweat lodge," says Joe. "We wouldn't say it if
it wasn't important."

In the evening darkness the students assemble in their
bathing suits (the Italians, of course, in virtual thong bikini
briefs). There is something strange and primal about this dis-
robed crowd in the moonlight. Their progress into the lodge is
slow, taking some time before they are all in. I can hear Brown
beginning his incantatory singing, and almost immediately I
see some people having to get out. From those who stayed
throughout the ceremony, I am told of moments of difficulty,
when sudden walls of heat made even getting one's next breath
difficult. Apparently this situation was not helped by the fact
that, despite Joe's proscription against flatulence, the sweat
lodge clearly brings it out in people. One man was seated behind such a pair who just couldn't help themselves. "It got
kind of bad there. I mean, they didn't let out any crackers or
anything, but one of them was a pretty significant one," he
says.

. . .

I rise early on the last morning. I'm almost the only student awake. I ask if there's anything I can do, and one of the volunteers asks me to build up the fire. Well, how the fuck am I supposed to do that? I think to myself. Almost as quickly, I realize I know precisely how to do that, and much more. I have never taken in more information in one week of my life. Can I track a mouse across a gravel driveway? I couldn't even track a mouse across a cookie sheet spread with peanut butter, but that's no matter. Despite Kevin's recantation in his final wrap-up, when he begs us, *"Don't* quit your jobs. Don't make any radical decisions for the next three months, don't trash your relationships." ("How many of us did *that?"* Ruth Ann stage-whispers.) I can't help feeling that I *could* if I needed to, and survive. Lavishly.

One of the other students gives me a lift to the bus station. I count the numerous roadkills on the shoulder of the highway. I could do something with that. And that. And that, I think. I resist the temptation to ask her to pull over and let me out, so that I may walk away from the car, part the trees, and step through, letting the branches close behind me as I keep going until I can no longer be seen from the road.

TOKYO STORY

"There's got to be lots of opportunities that we haven't explored for the kinds of lubricants that you supply," the American businessman on the bus from Narita airport says to his Japanese associate at the precise moment that we pass the sadly down at heel yet optimistically named Hotel Let's, the merest look at which demands the follow-up "not and say we did." With a sign that advertises different rates to "rest" and to "stay," the Let's is evidently one of Tokyo's many "love hotels," louche mainstays of both extramarital and connubial relations. Love hotels are looked upon benignly, as a fact of life in a city where living space is so limited.

Such oleaginous talk reminds me of the Tokyo of the 1980s, when I, with my college degree in Japanese studies in hand, moved there after graduation. It was at the height of Japan's world economic dominance, wistfully referred to as "the Bubble," although the epoch's bounty largely passed me by. I worked as a translator for an art publisher, gamely staying in a tiny room in a dicey neighborhood of love hotels like Charme, Maîtresse, and Le Refrain and subsisting on a daily diet of Mild Seven Lights cigarettes and the two hundred-gram box of chocolate-covered almonds from the subway kiosk.

I haven't been back since 1986 and haven't wanted to go back. Tokyo is the scene of my first, abortive attempt at an adult life. It was in Tokyo that the small pea-size lump in my neck grew with steady and alarming rapidity over the course of three short weeks until it was the size of a rather juicy plum, necessitating my defeated departure. Scarcely four months after lighting out for the territories, I was forced to return to Toronto, vanquished and sick; the young Turk cut off at the knees. Understandably, there is a lingering Waterlooish feeling about Tokyo.

I have accepted this assignment from a travel magazine reluctantly—I even turned it down once. I was worried about reliving some old trauma. Worried about, not to put too fine a point on it, losing my shit and bursting into tears on some foreign street corner, thousands of miles away from my home. I was also illogically convinced that returning to the scene of the crime would somehow prompt my lymph nodes to bloom forth into malignancy once more.

Finally facing down that demon, I have decided to hope instead that this trip will prove exculpatory, putting to rest once and for all that sense of unrequited love between Tokyo and myself. I am also hoping this visit, coinciding with the newly tanking Japanese economy, will mean that I will finally be able, indeed am enjoined, to savor the city in a way unavailable to me at the green and miserable age of twenty-two.

I have been inundated with gloomy anecdotal evidence of Japan's depression: tales of the legions of *risutora* (derived from the term *restructured,* the Japanese equivalent of our own oblique and sinister neologism "downsizing"), those individuals who, unable to tell their wives of their disemployment, daily put on their suits and leave their homes, only to spend the eight hours sitting in the parks or riding the subways. All of this has made my head swim with visions of a holiday spent like a pasha among scores of have-nots. *Lots* of opportunities for lubricants.

My abominable, grandiose fantasies are not remotely augured by my flight. Those of us in economy are so vastly outnumbered by first- and business-class travelers, they've curtained off the entire unused rear third of the plane. At least I have three seats to myself, all the better to watch a roistering comedy about a Tokugawa-period angling enthusiast, *Samurai Fishing Nut*. The hours pass like days.

Nor are Japan's economic woes outwardly visible as I walk out onto the Ginza of a Saturday evening in spring. Tokyo remains the city lover's paradise. The Ginza is still a vertiginous canyon of stores, blazing with neon in Angkor Wat profusion: *Blade Runner* directed by Dr. Seuss. The surreal quality is enhanced by having been awake for thirty hours, dropping my bags at my hotel, and taking a stroll in the purple twilight. On the front of the Warner Brothers store, a dubbed Tweety outsmarts Sylvester, only to be replaced moments later by quickly alternating images of Jennifer Aniston and the cast of *ER*. On another jumbotron down the block, a Godzilla-size Kim Basinger rubs some miracle emollient into her gargantuan pores. (The economy still seems strong enough to cough up sufficient mammon to pay American stars, too pure to do commercials domestically, to hawk wares in Japan. In the past it has been Woody Allen, Sylvester Stallone, and Kathleen Battle. On this trip, in addition to Ms. Basinger, I see ads with Leonardo DiCaprio and Kevin Costner.) The stores are full, the streets throng with young people. Even in the window of the Matsuya department store, the Issey Miyake Pleats Please sweaters, suspended on invisible wires, bounce up and down in accordioned, carefree bliss—so happy to be sportswear.

My feet, through some unconscious memory, lead me to the fondly remembered Ginza Lion Beer Hall. It's just as I recall, a lovely Teutonic vaulted interior in honey-colored glazed ceramic tile. It's like the clattery cafeteria at Valhalla. Over the bar is an Arcadian mosaic of Rhine maidens at harvest: toga-like garments, sheaves of grain, blond hair. The clientele is a mix of generations, from the very young to the youngish. I nurse my beer as I scan the crowd with rapidly dwindling comprehension, now thoroughly in the fugue state of jet lag. Is it really possible that they *all* have cell phones? (Yes, as it turns out.) The overriding sense of Tokyo—and I don't think an inaccurate one—is that it is a city devoted to the new, sped up in a subtle but profound way: a postmodern science-fiction story set ten minutes in the future.

Not that I would know anything about the future. I seem to have a negative aptitude for prediction. My first job in Tokyo in 1986 was one I held very briefly—twelve hours—with an advertising firm that was starting up a "computer network" where English-speaking expats could "log on" and "talk" to one another or get useful information from a "newsletter." This was all explained to me by Jeff, the only other Westerner in the company, a Montana native. Jeff sat me down and, with Pentecostal fervor, tried vainly to explain the mechanics of computers, drawing incomprehensible diagrams on a legal pad. I could not feign interest; indeed, I could barely stay conscious. I knew at that moment that this job would not work out. Talk to one another on the computer? I thought. What a bunch of losers. In my diary from that time, I find the entry where I talk about this "network": *Who* needs *something like this? Strictly for those comic book enthusiast weirdos who actually take the advice of those little boxes that read "for more on the Green Goblin, check out Spidey #137—Ed."*

Trying to make conversation, I pointed out how strange it was that on some level the newsletter didn't really exist.

"What do you mean?" Jeff snorted defensively.

The term *virtual* had not yet been coined then, at least not for the general population. This was the only remotely intelligent thing I said that day.

I was to spend my time looking at back issues of the publication, to get a feel for its readership. I was seated at a long table of computers beside three other Japanese men. Using my very first mouse, I moved it to the edge of its pad. The cursor shifted about three inches to the right across the screen and no farther. Rising from my chair, I continued to move the mouse down the table. On the screen, the cursor crawled another three inches to the right. Now at the elbow of the man beside me, I wordlessly showed him my screen, my stalled cursor, and pointed beyond his shoulder farther down the table, indicating my manifest destiny ever rightward.

Gently he picked up my mouse and showed me how to move it along and pick it up incrementally. "You must uplift the mouse," he said. Uplift the Mouse! *This* mouse, I decided, would never master it. It was time to free myself from the shackles of the job before things got ugly. I quit the next morning.

Walking out of that office, as buoyant as someone who's had his *Titanic* reservations canceled, I said to myself, *Sayonara,* suckers. Good luck with your *network.* Weeks later I was relieved to be making a barely living wage in book publishing.

Getting it slightly but disastrously wrong was my specialty that year. At the only wealthy expatriate party to which I was invited, I stood talking to a small circle of investment banker types, when the subject of the Mormon missionaries came up. One used to see them all over Tokyo, traveling around in pairs on bicycles, with their initially-handsome-and-then-not-really-on-closer-inspection blond faces, short-sleeved polyester white dress shirts, and dairy-fed fat asses.

"It seems unfair," said a young woman with Crédit Lyonnais. "Everything is so crowded in Tokyo, and they have no private space at all. I heard they even make them room together." We were in an apartment in the Akasaka district that was huge even by New York standards.

Her British Lazard Frères boyfriend explained, "Well, they do that so they can watch each other in case one of them is tempted to have a wank."

"Well," say I, drunk, twenty-two, smart-ass, "it's always better with someone watching."

This was my first and final encounter with Tokyo affluence.

Until now. The Seiyo is the first of three hotels that I will stay in over the next ten days. I decided that it would be a *really good idea* for the story (italics and *really stupid idea* my own) to mirror the Bubble and its aftermath by staying in progressively cheaper hotels. Come see the Human Economic Synecdoche! Thrill to the sight of his declining fortunes!

The Seiyo's quiet elegance, its second-floor lobby, subdued golden beige palate, is anodyne after the thrum outside. The intelligent, friendly, and bilingual staff keep their voices low, at the dulcet register of the museum gift shop. Even by Japanese standards they are solicitous. I ask one of the concierges a question in Japanese. He begins to answer me in English, then stops, apologizes, and switches to his native tongue.

My room is a riot of color: taupe, buff, sandstone, wheat, parchment, and cream. On the small side table sits a black lacquer tray with a small mountain of perfect strawberries, kiwi, thin-skinned oranges, and cherry-size plums, along with a personalized note of welcome. The toiletries in the bathroom are just the lubricants I was hoping for: the kinds of ridiculously silken unguents I would never buy for myself, including a cunning can of shaving cream the size of a piece of chalk. To merely say or even think the word *towel* at the Seiyo is to find one of the numerous huge bath sheets replaced. None of this should be a surprise, given the nightly expense of my room, which hovers somewhere around the monthly cost of my apartment. Although gratuities are not part of Japanese culture, I wonder briefly if the world of luxury at this level is beyond nationality, if the Seiyo, more than being in Tokyo, is some international principality, a consular outpost of the mythic land Affluencia, where tycoons and movie stars still "duke the help," to paraphrase Mr. Sinatra.

Half a block away from the hotel one morning a doorman, out of breath, taps me on the shoulder and hands me a beige (of course) pearwood-handled umbrella. I have risen, falsely refreshed, at four A.M., the international dateline playing havoc with my circadian rhythms. At that hour in Tokyo there's only one place to go: Tsukiji, the fish market where over 5 percent of the world's seafood is sold daily. Immediately outside the market stands a three-story mountain of white Styrofoam boxes. If I squint through the rainy mist, this snowy mound is as close to a convincing view of Fuji as I come over the next ten days.

And how astonishing is Tsukiji itself! It is so vast, of such volume, the brawn and biology of it so daunting, that it's like getting to see where they make air. Aisle after aisle of sea creatures: eels, octopi (in both charcoal and vivid carmine), cockles, clams, fish of all varieties, crimson roe, the tiniest fish I have ever seen—bright white, smaller than bobby pins with minuscule poppyseed black eyes—crabs, sea urchins, sardines, squid, which all give way to the open area known as *tekka jigoku,* Tuna Hell, where the prized fish are auctioned off. If unfathomable profusion be hell, then this Madison Square

Garden—size, wet, sodium-lit garage, shrouded in the mist wicking off the frozen tuna, is it. Small circles of men gather every few yards, crowding around the auctioneers who stand atop one of the iced, rock-hard beasts. Nothing prepares you for how big a tuna is. Easily the size of an English teacher, each one is labeled with red paint directly onto its silver skin, indicating where in the world's oceans it was caught. Near the tail, a small flap has been cut, to give prospective buyers a look at the flesh.

If you don't work there, Tsukiji is an exercise in being in the way. The aisles are almost impossibly narrow, and men barrel through on little motorized trucks with oil-drum-like steering mechanisms, making no concession to space or speed. Those on foot carry long fish gaffs, big meat hooks on wooden handles. It's amazing that the place isn't littered with the walking wounded, the gored, the run down, or run through by one of the long two-person saws used to cut up the frozen tuna.

"Do you speak Japanese? Because we don't speak English," I am greeted at the sushi bar I enter at seven A.M. The only Westerner in the tiny place, I sit between a young couple on my right, blissed out in morning afterglow, and to my left a scarily bright-eyed foursome of Prada-wearing businesspeople, two men, two women. I am given the choice of a $30 or a $23 breakfast set. Deciding upon the latter (even as I write this I am still stewed in regret over my foolishly saved ¥800), I begin with a miso soup flavored with thumbnail-size clams. The sushi—extraordinarily fresh, some pieces still eerily warm with recent life, others bracingly freezing—is placed directly on the counter in front of me.

Perhaps it's the early morning protein jolt of all that fish, the sheer Carl Sandburg big shoulders quality to the whole Tsukiji enterprise, or the proximity to all that top o' the food chain death and mayhem, but I leave exultant, walking out into the rain with a high heart like Gene Kelly.

My exuberance isn't entirely food related. I have been so relieved to find that the city in and of itself is not enough to unlock the sadness or fear of my younger self. To the contrary, I have been unable to wipe the smile from my face since I arrived, giddy with a sense of survival. It's not even clear to me that that old misery is still even housed in my body anymore. I had been avoiding a monster behind a door for thirteen years, only to find that it had melted away long ago, nothing more than a spun-sugar bogeyman. It's definitely not the first time in my adulthood that I have realized this, but it never fails to cheer me to have it proven yet again that almost any age is better than twenty-two.

An enormous blue balloon of *Dobbu-kun* ("Mr. DOB") artist Takashi Murakami's mouse-eared, agate-eyed Everycreature adorns the entrance to the Shinjuku branch of the Parco department store. Department stores are far more microcosmic than their American counterparts, with bookstores, food halls to rival Harrod's, and art galleries of important stature. Murakami is at the forefront of the Japanese vanguard that owes much to *anime* cartoons, *manga* (comics), and archetypal Japanese cuteness. Limited to neither the strawberry-scented eraser world of *Hello, Kitty* nor the ubiquitous youth-lobotomizing cult of Pika-chu and his Pokémon pals, the archetypal aesthetic of *kawai* ("cute," most often said in reference to a pencil case and drawn out in a nasal whine, almost pained at the intolerable levels of said object's adorability) now spans both the globe and generations, from schoolchildren to club kids to the worlds of typography and design. Mr. DOB's candy-colored world of smiling daisies and psychedelic toadstools is very *kawai* indeed, albeit with a vaguely sinister undertone of throbbing sexuality and atomic age anxiety. It has brought out the full range of Tokyo trendocrats: art students, critical theory heads, collectors. An American dealer in a blue blazer and Hermès tie walks from painting to painting, talking in Japanese into his cell phone. His pressed jeans are rolled up at the cuff, revealing the red thread at the selvage, the telltale proof that these are the limited-edition Levi's manufactured exclusively for the denim-mad Japanese market.

In terms of sheer label-crazed consumerism, the Japanese have always been able to teach Americans a thing or two. I walk through Takeshita-dori, a rabbit warren of streets and alley-ways geared to the city's younger adolescents: teens in their autonomy training wheels phase. It is a crush of juvenile bodies, many in school uniforms—the girls wearing their trademark *ruusu soksu* (literally "loose socks"), white socks that grip the leg just below the knee and then cascade in folds of ribbed cotton, pooling over and around their shoes. The river of youth flows in and out of stores selling notebooks, lighters, stickers, pens, and clothing that will come apart after one washing—all the merchandise is eye-catching and fairly shitty, the entire scene scored with incredibly loud bubblegum music.

All of this buzz, both aural and visual, is vibrant but leaves me feeling clobbered. Seeking out an antidote to all the stimulus, I board the subway. I can only sympathize with the man in suit and tie (perhaps one of those fabled *risutora?* I shall never know) dozing with his sleeping four-year-old daughter. Tied around the father's wrist is a plastic bag in which a goldfish— not asleep—swims casually back and forth. I am bound for my favorite part of Tokyo, Yanaka and Nippori, two adjacent neighborhoods that are part of Tokyo's old Shitamachi (downtown). The myth that Tokyo's history has been effaced by earthquake and war is, thankfully, only partially true. Yanaka is marked by its authentic working-class flavor, old houses, profusion of lovely temples, and magnificent cemetery. The

main shopping strip is a narrow pedestrian mall of food stores
and utilitarian shops, grandly named, in a touching bit of
puffery, the Yanaka Ginza. I buy a small bag of fish balls from a
vendor and walk along snacking in one of the few areas of
Tokyo where public eating is not a faux pas. A politician running in the current municipal elections stands beside his
idling station wagon, addressing a small group of shoppers
and merchants. He finishes to a smattering of applause and
gets back in his car. All around town I see entire walls plas-
tered with posters for dozens of candidates. Later on in the day
the rain graduates to full-on torrential as the same candidate,
getting soaked, promises all manner of things that I cannot understand to me and two 7-year-old schoolchildren on their way
home. I stand listening, too embarrassed to move.

Yanaka cemetery is as crowded with headstones as Père
Lachaise, only the markers, rather than being adorned with
crosses, are festooned with *sotoba,* wooden pickets painted with
the decedent's Buddhist name in kanji. The lanes are sodden
with rain, the paths muddy. Huge ravens, oily black, sit soaked
and spindle feathered in the bare trees. It is blessedly still, inordinately peaceful, and contemplative. I am alone here, even
though I am in central Tokyo, a stone's throw from the railroad tracks of the train station, a short ride from my hotel. A
good thing, too. In ten days I never manage to sleep more than
four hours at a time, so I return to the hotel each afternoon for
a very necessary rest and some even more necessary TV
watching.

Television is good practice for my remaining Japanese, a
mere fingernail paring of comprehension and conversational
ability. TV is also my only indication that Tokyo is no longer
Fat City. I see a number of new shows concerned with "bar-
gains." The camera careering through a grocery store as the
hostess holds up packages of sea urchin for only ¥350! She is
amazed! A restaurant in Nagoya serves curry rice (a Japanese

staple: a brown, curry-scented gravy of dubious provenance
served over rice) for only ¥1! The patrons shoveling the mess
into their mouths are most definitely getting what they pay
for. On another program, a housewife economizes by making
everything by hand: the family tofu, the potato chips. She has
ledger books and calculators. I watch her attend a pot luck,
having managed to keep the cost of her ample contribution
down to ¥30. At the end of the taped sequence, in the studio
audience with her husband and two children, she is presented
with a certificate of accomplishment. Her nerves worn fila-
ment thin from her labor, she bursts into tears.

There is also the equal and opposite reaction to all this fru-
gality. High Life programs with host after host going to hot
springs hotels. After being shown in the bath discreetly naked,
they lounge in cotton *yukata* robes by a hibachi. A large clam is
placed directly over the flame and pops open, the rilled edges
of the creature furling in succulent demise—a time-lapse
flower in reverse. I see this image at least three times.

The only person with whom I have maintained barely sporadic
contact in the decade-plus since I lived in Japan is Kyoko
Makino, with whom I worked at the art publisher. When I go to
pick her up for dinner, I feel none of the anticipated trepidation as I walk into the office. I know almost nobody still working at the publishing house, and I, in turn, am barely
remembered. The new publisher is the son of the man I
worked for. When he was nineteen to my twenty-two, I tutored
him in English. Even though it is quite clear that I am there to
see Makino-*san* and not him, he sends her off to get me some
coffee that I do not want. After ushering me into the conference room, he shows me the company's newest project, a magazine devoted to oenophilia in Japan. (This will prompt me
later over dinner to teach Makino-*san* the term *wine bore*.)

We have come to a restaurant in an old house at the end of a long, shaded walkway, lit with glowing braziers. We sit on tatami, an ember-filled grill in the center of our table. A seemingly endless variety of beautiful dishes emerges from the kitchen, starting with three small rectangles of tofu on bamboo skewers, each block enameled with a puree of a different color—green pea, orange squash, and a vermilion sweet miso— and ending some two hours later with a chilled slice of Japanese melon, dark jade and nearly translucent. The meal is extraordinary, and we spend a great amount of time talking about how good everything is. "Isn't this sort of the same thing as a 'wine bore'?" Kyoko asks. "Are we being a 'food bore'?" Scandalized by such a ridiculous suggestion, I assure her we are no such thing.

Night falls. I look out through the shoji into the central courtyard. There are two smaller teahouses, used as private dining rooms, the stone steps up to each of them ensnared in wisteria roots. It is a perfect evening. For many reasons, actually. Japanese is the unbicycle of languages: you *never* remember, and I had been fearing that my speech, unpracticed for over a decade, coupled with stereotypical Japanese reserve would confine Makino-*san* and myself to such conversational gambits as "Oh, look, beer!" and "Yes!" But I have remembered a great deal more than I thought. We talk about former co-workers, marriage and singlehood, aging parents, all of the things I might talk about with friends in New York.

This greater openness of feeling is true of almost all my encounters. The Bubble, with its influx of foreign business, has achieved what over a century's passage—since Japan first opened up to the West at the beginning of the Meiji period in 1868—and even a postwar occupation could not accomplish: Tokyoites seem almost completely inured to Westerners, thanks in part to the scores of foreigners I see speaking perfect, unhalting Japanese. By the same token, the use of egregiously bad English is also far less in evidence, although happily has not entirely died out, as evidenced by the T-shirt on sale in the Melrose Boutique for Men that reads, simply: "Blow jobs $10." At around 118 yen to the dollar, this would be one of the city's real bargains. Actually the city's real bargain is the once legendarily expensive Tokyo coffee. I keep reminding myself that it is we who have caught up with Japan, now that "Double Skinny Macchiato" has become global Esperanto for "Here's my savings, where's my breakfast?"

Here is the object lesson of room 201 of the Tokyo Station Hotel, my second place of lodging: the time that it takes to utter, in camp appreciation, "This room is like a set from a snuff film. It's faaabulous!" also turns out to be the maximum amount of time one really wants to stay in same. It is another matter entirely to have to sleep there for two nights. It is very high ceilinged and enormous, but room 201 is the kind of sad interior where gamblers down on their luck live out their last days, only to end up drunkenly falling against the sharp corner of the coffee table, scattering their pills across the nylon carpet, and slowly bleeding to death. Not a happy place. Although clean, the place is grimy with disrepair and shabbiness: overhead fluorescent lighting, chipped wood veneer, and antimacassars on the armchairs, worn shiny with use and old pomade. And what can one say about a room where everything is so meticulously and ostentatiously wrapped for "your sanitary protection"? That old witticism of the schoolyard "Whoever smelt it, dealt it" springs to mind.

My previous hotel certainly didn't feel the need to protest this much. Whereas at the Seiyo, in the dresser drawer, along with the stationery and room service menus, there was also, beautifully printed on vellum, a suggested jogging route around the Imperial Palace gardens, at the Tokyo Station Hotel I am provided with a long list of "Rules on

Accommodation Utilization." I am told "not to give annoy-
ance to others by making great noise or disgusting behaviors."
I am forbidden from bringing onto the premises "things with
loathsome smell" and, inexplicably, "materials in great quan-
tity." But for the omission of "Don't Shoot the Piano Player,"
it is a code of conduct straight out of Dawson City. I am also
proscribed from "hanging up such items at the windows which
will spoil the outside view of this hotel." While it is true that
the Tokyo Station Hotel from the front is a lovely red-brick-
and-limestone building like the great railway hotels of old,
should I choose to open the pebbled-glass windows of 201,
which faces the back, I would be greeted with a view of the permanent dusk from the elevated track above, the hum of indus-
trial air ducts below, and at eye level, not twenty feet away, a
commuter platform, complete with salary man looking
straight back at me. I have often wondered, when riding into
cities late at night on the train, Who are the sad people behind
those darkened windows that directly abut the tracks? Now, in
some small measure, I know.

I couldn't feel sorrier for myself. Don't they know I'm fragile? After a scant four days of the betoweled lushness of the
Seiyo, I have turned into the high-maintenance jerk of my own
worst nightmares. Fleeing my room, I seek out the city's nocturnal diversions.

I eat supper at an outdoor yakitori restaurant, a stall with
chairs and two tiny tables, underneath the highway overpass
near Yuraku-cho station. The sidewalk and traffic are barely
masked by the *noren,* the abbreviated curtains that hang down
a foot or so. In the rain, right up against the traffic, both foot
and vehicular, drinking my beer while I wait for my food, I am
overcome with the urban romance of it all. How, I wonder, is it
all that different from my high-ceilinged hotel room, disinfec-
ted for my comfort and protection, that sits right up against
the railroad tracks, waiting for me?

Not ready to go back there just yet, I hop the train to Ebisu,

Tokyo's youth Mecca ascendant. The holdup at the door to Milk, one of the city's most popular clubs, is not so management can verify ID, frisk for weapons, or confiscate drugs. It is due to the many umbrellas being checked by the young, *young* crowd. Sporting my natural hair color and not wearing whiteframed Lina Wertmuller sunglasses makes me stand out almost as much as my being one of the only Westerners on line, not to mention being a good ten years older than everyone else. Upon entering, a nineteen-year-old girl in baby barrettes, a T-shirt worn over a sweater, and orange canvas clam diggers presses something small and round into our palms. Ah, I think, holding the disk-shaped freebie, good old condoms. I look down and see that we have been handed not rubbers, but rather six plastic bookmarks printed with the prim slogan "Yes, I do, but not with you."

Milk doesn't seem all that much different from most clubs I've been to. It is loud, dark, crowded, underserviced by toilets. A Japanese thrash band plays, the lead singer adorably shirtless and screaming. Young men boil around like piranhas in the mosh pit. I am no more inclined to join them now than I was a decade ago, but I can always use a good bookmark.

Returning late to room 201, I muster sufficient Japanese to say to the night clerk at the hotel, "My room is making me very sad. I would like to kill myself. May I have a different one tomorrow, facing the front, perhaps?" And so off to bed, feeling spoiled and venal. The room is quiet and dark, at least, the platform outside my window silent and closed for the night. I bless the fact that the city's mass transit stops just after twelve, with the exception of one night a year, December 31, when they run all night.

On New Year's Eve the already mythically crowded Tokyo subways are exponentially more so. During normal rush hour the *tsukebe,* Tokyo's storied subway *frotteurs,* can at least find enough space to get their grubby hands on the nether parts of some poor unsuspecting girl; on New Year's Eve you literally cannot move. You just hope you've gotten on the same car as enough people going to the same stop as you; otherwise you will have to wait until the river of humanity decides to disembark.

Early on January 1, 1987, my evening's celebration concluded, the dawn of a new year breaking, I stood on just such a train. It was a function of how blitzed I was from the night's revels, traveling from shrine to temple to club, drinking all the while, that I didn't experience a complete agoraphobic attack. As we approached my stop, I looked over to my right. There, not eight feet away, was a young woman, jammed up facing a man about a head taller than she. He began that unmistakable wet-mouthed, lip-smacking, compulsive swallowing that indicates the impending need to vomit. His upper lip shone with perspiration, and his eyes were closed. The woman had nowhere to go—indeed, there was nothing she would be able to do until the train reached the station, and that might not be in sufficient time. If the first thing you do on the first day augurs the spirit and tone of your new year, this woman was in for a very bad 1987. She began to cry.

In one of those vodka-pure moments of proof that laughter is often nothing more than anxious release—I, on the other hand, began to giggle uncontrollably. The joke was on me, of course, because I ended up having the shitty year.

The Hotel Alcyone, next stop on my ever-downward spiral, is scrupulously clean. Even the carpets in the elevator are changed daily, because like the panties from Bloomingdale's 1970s Forty Carrots heyday, they are printed with "Sunday, Monday," and so on. My room is undeniably monastic, however. Small and Spartan, and again, while clean, it seems academic if one can't actually distinguish between something that is dirty and something that merely looks dirty. But at under $100 a night near the Ginza, it is an affordable, well-located bargain, if not a tad gloomy. Sitting on my bed before I go out for my last evening in Tokyo, I experience the first earth tremor of the trip. As much a feeling as a noise, a deep, all-encompassing, almost electric rumbling. It lasts only a very few seconds, but I think, How perfect to buy the farm here at the Hotel Alcyone, flattened and crushed, this sprung mattress with its Hollofil polyester bedspread my funeral bier.

Later that evening I eat roasted eel in the top-floor restaurant of a department store in Shinjuku. The restaurant is famous for its eel. The traditional accompaniment to *unagi* is green *sansho* (mountain pepper) powder. I have been warned that taking too much will make my "tongue go to sleep." I take too much. It tastes of concentrated citrus peel with an intermittently forceful salty note and something green underneath, like hyssop. Sure enough, my lips start to buzz, my tongue and throat feel as if they are lined with Velcro. The sensory strangeness is amplified terrifyingly by the evening's second earth tremor, stronger than the first and eight seconds long. Try it right now: sit for eight seconds and imagine the very ground shifting, unstable, threatening immediate and lethal liquefaction. But the eel is really delicious.

Close to midnight I find myself in a near empty plaza underneath an enormous outdoor television screen. I stand, rapt, among five or six homeless men and a small crowd of young people, their telephones quiet for the moment, as we watch an extended Nescafé commercial: a thrilling montage of people of various ages, races, and genders falling in love in fields, farmhouses, cafés, churches. "Open up!" sings the song, urging us to embrace the world in all its romantic, universal, caffeinated glory.

Perhaps "Open up" really means the ground will continue

its tremors, forming fissures that widen and swallow whole this extraordinary, illusory city. God knows I once felt the specter of obliteration here before, a destruction from which I thought I'd never recover, and the ground hadn't had to move an inch. For now, though, the only thing shaking is my two hundred-gram box of chocolate-covered almonds. I am becalmed by the sound that I have quite a few left.

I USED TO BANK HERE, BUT
THAT WAS LONG, LONG AGO

Hodgkin's disease, the illness that sent me packing from Tokyo at the age of twenty-two, is a form of lymphatic cancer, common among young men in their twenties. Hodgkin's is also highly curable. So highly curable, in fact, that I like to refer to it as the dilettante cancer.

An old Canadian joke bears telling here: A boss says to an underling, "I'm off to Sault Sainte Marie for the weekend."

"Sault Sainte Marie?" asks the employee, incredulous. "But, boss, there are only whores and hockey players in Sault Sainte Marie."

"My wife is from Sault Sainte Marie."

"Oh. (*beat*) What position does she play?"

When I joke about Hodgkin's being the cancer for boys who do things in half measures, it is invariably to someone whose husband or brother or son has just died from Hodgkin's. I don't mean to denigrate other survivors or less fortunate nonsurvivors. My inappropriate wisecrack only serves to prove a point about myself. On some level, despite the fact that I received both radiation and chemotherapy, I cannot escape the feeling that I was, at best, a cancer tourist, that my survival means I dabbled. Kinda been there, sorta done that. It has only recently occurred to me that perhaps I might stop glibly insisting that the cancer wasn't real and the doctors popped me into an Easy-Bake Oven, where a forty-watt light bulb halted the metastasis in its tracks.

What remains, almost fourteen years after the fact? Four small tattoos, subcutaneous black dots, like compass points on my torso; near total numbness in the very tips of my fingers, as well as a palm-size area on my right inner thigh also without feeling; some dry mouth; and, most lastingly, three straws of my prechemotherapized sperm, in cold storage, somewhere in Toronto. Like millions of tiny Walt Disneys, they wait, frozen, until the day I will return and have them conjoined with some willing ovum and thereby fulfill their zygotic destiny, growing into children who will eventually go on to break my heart and not talk to me.

I'm not entirely sure I even want children of my own, although I'd like to keep my options open. Being of a certain class and living in Manhattan, I have been led to believe that my life is nothing but an embarrassment of options. Parenthood frequently comes late around these parts. Go to any playground on the Upper West Side, and you will find that most of the grown-ups are fortyish, and among the children there is an overrepresentation of fertility treatment— enhanced sets of twins and adopted Chinese girls. Once, I watched as a twenty-eight-year-old mother arrived at the jungle gym with her toddler. Twenty-eight might even be considered late for a new mother elsewhere in these United States, but there she looked like some Appalachian child bride, ridiculously young for the burden of parenthood. Everybody was casting concerned glances her way, as if to ask, "Who is the brute who did this to you?"

So it's more than a simple desire for kids—who can be fairly boring, truth be told. I just want to know where the sperm is. Easier said than done, as it turns out, because since that time, I have moved, my parents have moved, the sperm bank has moved, and the cancer hospital has moved. The traces have been thoroughly kicked over, which suits me fine. I'm not by nature terribly sentimental. I'm not a photo taker, I have no scrapbooks, I have attempted to never look back, until now.

Along with my scar, my tattoos, and my numbness, these straws of sperm are the only things I have left from that time in my life, a period of eighteen months that I have generally tried to not think about. At the age of thirty-five I'm starting to feel that it's bad juju to continue to ignore it. So I am off to find the straws, just in time for their microscopic bar mitzvahs.

My decision to write about my quest is as much about providing myself with a welcome screen of white noise as it is about any need for documentation. My clutching a notebook while searching for the perfect one-liner will be a comfortable distraction from what might result in my feeling something, which is never my first choice.

I was treated at PMH: the Princess Margaret Hospital, the main cancer facility in Toronto. If you were a child at any time from the 1930s through the 1950s, living anywhere in the British empire, chances are you were inundated with images of the two young princesses, Elizabeth and Margaret. Elizabeth would eventually become queen, of course, but Margaret was always considered to be somewhat prettier, and simply by virtue of her thwarted ascendancy to the throne, she was less duty-bound and consequently more fun. Kicky, almost. As she grew up and had her serial doomed romances, Margaret gave the Commonwealth public a taste of the kind of low-rent scandal we could later come to expect from the house of Windsor.

It's not as if she was a slattern or an embarrassment. Calling it the Princess Margaret Hospital is not like naming it the Billy Carter. It's more affectionate than that, more glamorous: the Tricia Nixon might be more apt.

The harvesting of sperm before chemotherapy is a fairly standard practice. Chemo makes you sterile. They suggest it to most male patients of a certain age. It is certainly the most important sperm sample I have ever given, but it is not the first. In 1982, as a freshman, I sold it once. Every bulletin board in my dormitory on 114th Street and Amsterdam Avenue had the following flyer: "College Men! Make Money Now!" It was an advertisement for a midtown sperm bank. We would be paid close to fifty dollars to do, under somewhat more controlled circumstances, the very thing that was occupying a great deal of our waking lives anyway. The lab was very interested in our seed: the Sperm of the Ivy League. There's something so obscenely vital, so borderline eugenic, about that image, imbued with a potency and a Riefenstahlian vision of the future. It was a stereotype much greater than the actual sum of its parts, I can assure you, given some of the knock-kneed Hebrews I went to school with, myself included. The lab wanted a fine-boned lacrosse player with a thatch of blond hair and a trust fund. What they got were pigeon-chested wiseacres who hardly belonged in that febrile pantheon of porn archetypes: the Cop Who Might Be Convinced Not to Write a Ticket; the Frustrated Repairman in Need of a Hand; the Pizza Boy Deserving of a Tip Yet Strangely Enough Not Carrying Any Change; and me for that brief afternoon in that small room with an acoustic tile ceiling, under fluorescent lights: the Strapping College Boy in the Examination Room (*Hey, Coach, I think I pulled a muscle in my groin*).

I remember nothing from that day. I cannot tell you if there were dirty magazines, although I suspect there were. I cannot remember being embarrassed, although I'm sure I was, and I cannot remember what I was paid, although forty dollars cash rings a bell. The conflation of climax and commerce cannot have failed to escape my notice. At age seventeen, it felt like sexual transgression. I suppose it still does, since until this story I have never told anyone about it.

Hanging on the wall on the way to the radiation room in the old hospital was a photograph of Princess Margaret's hand, taken on the occasion of the inauguration of the building. It was actually an X-ray photograph, so Her Highness's jewelry glows white against the bones and the vaporous gray of her invisible flesh. I look at it every time I go for treatment.

The radiation room itself is a lead-lined interior chamber of the hospital. Two red laser beams cross over the exact center of the table where the patients lie. Using the cross of four small black tattoos on my torso, the technicians line me up and ready me for the thousands of rads of radiation.

The machine is bulbous, huge, and a dull hospital green. A death ray straight out of fifties sci fi. I lie down and look up. Above my head, directly at eye level, someone has drawn a hastily rendered happy face in red marker. Underneath that is written the message "Give Us a Smile!" As with Rita Hayworth's picture that graced the side of the atom bomb they dropped on Bikini atoll, there's something so pathetic, so vastly outmatched, about this little happy face; a garnish on annihilation. Still, I never fail to smile. Even when I reach the point in the treatments when most of my hair has fallen out and my throat has been burned to such an extent that I cannot swallow, I smile.

They haven't stopped at the happy face, either. Every time the lead door closes, latching with a booming clank, so too begins the music. The same song every time. The same place in the same song every time: the full horn section buildup to the chorus of the song "You're Just Too Good to Be True." The plutonium drops down into the central cone, a warm wind starts to blow on my chest, indicating that I'm now getting the equivalent of a lifetime's worth of the recommended dose of gamma radiation. And I smile.

It's not all that hard, after all, to locate the missing sperm lab. A few phone calls and I find that it has been moved, lock, stock, and barrel, to another, more centrally located hospital. When I finally call them up directly to see if they still have my straws, they know all too well who I am. Like cops who spend a lifetime chasing a fugitive who, tired of years of running, gives up and turns himself in, the folks at the sperm bank taste the victory of finally nabbing a long-sought quarry; they've been waiting for me. Or, more precisely, for my money. There are apparently years of storage fees outstanding. I owe close to a thousand dollars. My account was years in arrears and re-ferred to collection. What would have happened if I had never checked up on this? Would I one day be walking past some pawnshop in Toronto and there in the window, next to the watches, the saxophone, and the old Canadian Legion of Honor war medallions, see three straws of my semen, thawing out in a dusty shaft of sunlight?

The folks at the lab view me with suspicion, but not because I am a Deadbeat Dad. What the folks at the lab are (rightfully) disquieted by is my need to frame my resurfacing as a story. They don't really understand why I want to tell it. They see my return and even the accrual of the debt—something that I have taken full responsibility for—as an indictment of them. "But we sent you bills!" the nursing manager says defensively when I am no more than thirty seconds into introducing myself on the phone. She's absolutely right, and I don't deny it. I vaguely recall receiving a bill in my old apartment and ignor-ing it. That was at a time in my life when I didn't want to know or remember anything about that year. If anyone's to blame for the trail having gone cold, I am, and I fully stipulate to this charge.

But my mea culpa is not enough to penetrate the chilly officiousness of the lab. They don't seem to want to talk to me. They are not interested in providing me with fodder for what they clearly see as a very fishy expedition. I try to ingratiate myself. In appealing to their sympathetic natures, I am reduced to using icky tricks, preambling each phone call by describing myself as having been "a cancer patient," talking about my need for "closure," and so forth. All of which seems a little melodramatic to me and leaves them almost completely unmoved anyway. Or, if I'm not being treacly, I'm playing the ridiculous schlemiel, stammering and apologizing: Lucy Ricardo losing Little Ricky while out shopping. It all leaves me with a bad taste in my mouth.

I am finally thrust into that long-sought movie scenario "Things were fine in this town before that *writer* showed up!" and I'm not sure I like it. They smell a rat, and that rat is me. What begin as frosty but cordial relations between the nursing manager and myself devolve steadily. By the time I fly to Toronto, she refuses to speak with me outright. I am Scrooge revisiting Christmas past, walking through a room, trying to right a wrong, and being completely unheard and unable to physically materialize. I will be able to pay the balance of storage fees, but I will not be able to see the facility, tour the vault or wherever it is they keep the straws, or ask her my many medical questions. My audience with the sperm of the Ivy League is denied.

I am now referred to a woman who works in the corporate communications department of the hospital that houses the sperm bank. She is to be my liaison. "Your project sounds really *innaresting?*" the PR woman tells me. "But I'm sorry we can't help you with it. If I can be of any further assistance, please don't hesitate to call me."

I was once employed in corporate communications. As a

framer of official meaning for someone else's mouth, I often used that very phrase in the name of my superiors: "If I can be of any further assistance, please don't hesitate to call me." But I never had the temerity to use it when I hadn't actually been of some assistance to begin with.

I recall the last time I saw these fugitive children of mine. It was in the summer of 1987. By that time my illness was fairly advanced, I was some thirty-five pounds underweight: an old man at the age of twenty-three. Virtually the last thing on my mind was onanism. I had been told if I could get the sample downtown to the lab within forty-five minutes, I could do the "harvest" at home. To this end, the lab technician at the sperm bank had given me some sterile containers. In the abstract, this sounded far more comfortable, producing my sample in the privacy of my childhood bedroom.

But privacy isn't really the name of the game when your mother has to drive you to the hospital. I have never been licensed by a sitting government to drive a car, and I am far too weak to take public transport. By happy coincidence, my mother's office is two blocks away from the hospital. It is a precisely timed operation. After breakfast she says to me euphemistically, "I'm going to start the car. Why don't you go upstairs and *get ready?*"—emphasis and winking italics my own. If this freaks her out, she doesn't let on. She's a physician herself, so it might just seem par for the course to tell your youngest child to go upstairs and salute the archbishop and then join you in the car.

My deed done, not my finest effort after what has arguably been half a lifetime of practice, I put on my coat and grab the jar. It is made of clear plastic. In college, my friend's parents came to New York for a psychoanalysts' convention. Getting onto a hotel elevator, crowded with their colleagues, my friend turned to his mother and stage-whispered, "Jocasta, I want you." But it is just me and my mother in the car. There are no Freudians to entertain with the discomfort of the Oedipal situation. Even in my weakened state, I'm certainly not going to ride next to my mother with a transparent vial of spooge in my lap. I look around the kitchen for a suitable bag and find the perfect one. It is four by six, of white paper. It has clearly been in the kitchen since I was very young, because when I turn it over I see that it's printed with the image of an orange pumpkin and a black cat and, in dripping, blood-soaked calligraphy, the words *Trick or Treat.*

I fly up to Toronto on a gray day in January of the new century, visiting, for the first time, the new Princess Margaret facility. It is beautiful, occupying an old art deco insurance building. It is imposing and elegant and graced in the center with a soaring six-story atrium. It is nothing like the old hospital where I was treated. I feel a little jealous as I walk in. There is even a multifaith chapel, which I don't recall from the old place. Outside of it, on a white board, someone on staff has written: "Just a thought:" and then a quote: "Joy is not in things, it is in us." It is attributed to one Robert Wagner, whose dates are 1813 to 1883. Presumably this is a different Robert Wagner from the wattle-concealing, turtleneck-wearing star of *The Towering Inferno* and *Hart to Hart.* So different a Robert Wagner, in fact, that when I try to look him up in my *Bartlett's Quotations,* he is not listed. Who *is* listed there, with exactly the same dates, however, is Richard Wagner, he of the proto-Nazi operas of heroic *übermenschen.* This puts a decidedly different spin on this little homily. And, funnily enough, *Bartlett's* doesn't list this lovely caveat against materialism among the composer's notable quotes. But it's a lot more suitable for an oncology chapel, after all, than "To be German means to carry on a matter for its own sake," don't you think? This new place is completely devoid of anything I might recall. Not a single doctor who treated me still works here. All along the front hallway are framed pictures of hospital directors past, my oncologist among them. Like most official portraits in oils, it misses something essential about the person. Now he just looks benignly Olympian and creamy. In the entrance is an official royal portrait of Her Royal Highness Princess Margaret. Taken recently—in 1998, according to the frame—she wears a gown of mushroom-colored satin, adorned with jeweled medals. And of course, being a real princess, she wears a crown. But the truly stunning feature, the one that announces to the world that we should not for an instant confuse her with her dowdy older sister, is Margaret's hair, a startling shade of brown-black. The unrelieved shock of too-youthful darkness over her not unattractive face of a certain age has turned her otherwise friendly smile into a toothy leer, that last tenuous stage of propriety before full-blown laughter at a dirty joke. It makes her look what used to be called "fast." Behold another porn archetype: the Randy Divorcée, lingering at her front door, swirling the ice cubes in her midday highball, saying to the strapping gardener, "You must be tired and sweaty after all that yardwork. C'mon in and cool off in the air-conditioning."

As for the fondly remembered X-ray photograph of her hand, it is nowhere to be seen. I ask the volunteer at the desk if they brought it here from the old facility.

"It was on the way to radiation," I say.

"I was also a radiation patient," she replies. "I don't remember it." She is apologetic. I then ask her if she remembers the music during treatment. She doesn't dismiss my recollection, but she's not sure herself, it was so long ago. All memory is porous. Details can change or go missing entirely, particularly in moments of physical peril. A kind of amnesia goes hand in hand with sickness, and a good thing, too. But of these two details—that X-ray photograph, that music—I am sure.

I think.

Since no one official or medical will talk to me at the sperm bank and I don't know anyone anymore at the cancer hospital, I spend the better part of two days hanging around the atrium. No one pays me any mind. When I look up I can see that the railings on the floors above are shielded with Plexiglas about eight feet high, well over the head of any potentially suicidal patient. Not long prior to my trip, I had a drink in a hotel with a huge atrium that goes up at least thirty stories. I asked the waitress if people ever pitched themselves over the sides in what would be a very public and punishing death, landing with a viscous splat at the patent-leather Mary Janed feet of a little girl on her way to her first Broadway show. The waitress seemed so bored, so in hate with her job, that when she answered my question with, "Yeah, thirteen people so far," there was an almost wistful tone in her voice, as though a falling body might just break up the monotony of her day.

Paradoxically, here at the cancer hospital things are decidedly cheerier. I walk back and forth, I listen to an extremely good jazz quartet playing the lunchtime concert. All hospitals are built around waiting. I don't stand out. In my year and a half of treatment at Princess Margaret, eighteen months of waiting, I never once saw anything that could have remotely been described as attitude. Not one patient, patient's guardian, partner, or parent ever got pissy that I could see. And I'll go out on a limb here and say that in the world of cancer it's not inconceivable that someone might have a right to feel like being at least a little pissy.

It might speak to that stereotypical Canadian reserve, but I choose to see it a little more heroically and politically. When medicine is socialized, when you have true universal health care, when everyone's treatment is the same regardless of socioeconomic station, those strong-arming attitudes of entitlement just aren't part of the vocabulary. This atrium, this lovely space in a hospital with a world-class reputation, is actually the equivalent of a state hospital. That American sense that someone somewhere else is getting what you're not, and the attendant demands that go along with that perceived injustice, well, it's just not in the equation here.

I've recently been told there is a chance that so many years after cure, my fertility might have rebounded. I decide to get tested back in New York, if only to stop having to pay the storage fees on my old sample. My friend Scott, who, for other reasons, was getting tested around that time, told me stories about the comfort and sheer titillation of the lab he went to: armchairs, privacy, pornography of every stripe; a masturbatorium, he called it. Maybe it's an insurance thing, because at the Upper East Side lab I go to, I am given a plastic vial, a Ziploc bag imprinted with the international symbol for biohazard, that vaguely sinister trillium, and pointed to the bathroom. It is directly off the reception area.

Have you ever been a temp, or in your first week in a new job, and right outside your cubicle your new office-mates hold a birthday party for one of their number? Do you remember how alienating and strange and embarrassing and generally impeding of your performance that birthday party was? I am the only patient in the lab that morning and the only man in the place. Through the door I can hear the technicians talking about their weekends, the scratch of the receptionist's ball-point as she fills out a magazine quiz, the crisp turning of a glossy page. This feels very public. To add to my difficulties, the bathroom is a standard-issue interior with very little to jog the mind. I peek out through the slats of the metal blinds on the window; maybe I can find a construction site or something to focus on. Nothing doing.

In the end, species will out, and I manage. Sheepishly I leave my sample at the front counter and leave. Why must everything be clear plastic?

The average fertile thirty-five-year-old man has many million sperm, a few million of which are motile enough to knock someone up. When I get my results, I find that I have ten. Not ten million: ten. Three are dead in the water, and the other seven are technically motile but given a grade very close to dead. I'm shooting blanks, as they say.

"Hey, at least you're shootin' 'em," says my doctor.

I come up with the idea of naming them. For all the male-of-the-species reproductive good they'll do me, I consider calling them all Janet. Then I settle on Radcliffe, Barnard, Bryn Mawr, Wellesley, Mount Holyoke, Smith, and Vassar.

Among my destinations on my trip up to Toronto is the site of the old hospital. I'm told it's being used now as a homeless shelter. It was in one of Toronto's few rubby-dub neighborhoods. There were a lot of hookers and also a Christian television ministry back when I was a patient.

The area has clearly been cleaned up, because I can't see

any hookers or visibly Christian folks, either. And the purported homeless people going into the old Princess Margaret
all look like backpacking northern Europeans. Perhaps it's a
hostel. I stand in the circular driveway, the place where the
smoking patients used to congregate with their IV stands and
enjoy their last fuck-it-all-to-hell cigarettes. I think of that
song "This Used to Be My Playground."

I'm trying to actually feel something about the whole thing
as I stand there, but I'm not really coming up with anything.
The building is possibly one of the more important structures
in my life. I feel I should well up with some sort of nostalgic
yearning, mourning my youth, anything. But it's just not happening, which is very strange. Or not.

Once, on my way home from radiation, a man came running out of the Knights of Columbus chapter near the hospital. Another man came running after him and, like a cartoon
panel come to life, the man giving chase actually yelled, "Stop,
thief!" I remember thinking to myself, Well, that's very cliché.
I was close to the robber. I could have stuck my foot out and
tripped him, perhaps. But I didn't. He made it across the
street, dodging traffic, and was out of sight in a moment. The
man from the Knights of Columbus stood frustrated on the
sidewalk as the cars rushed by. He turned and gave me a dirty
look for my inaction. I wanted to say something. I wanted to
explain how weak and tired and sick I was at that point. But
more than that, how I had essentially let go of any sense of
agency. I could lie on a table, they could shoot me full of
gamma rays, I would eat what was put in front of me, the hair
could fall from my head, my throat could be burned. But I was
not involved; I was a stranger here. That he could even see me
standing there seemed vaguely surprising.

The week before I moved back to New York, after having
finished chemotherapy, I went back to the ward to thank the
nurses for saving my life. To aid me in expressing my grati-

tude, I took them some chocolates. Good ones. Hard centers. No chart on the inside lid. I showed them the surgery scar from the final extraction of a burned-out lymph node from my abdomen. I thanked them, we all cried.

As a prophylactic against nausea, I had always gone to chemotherapy having taken an Ativan, a divine tranquilizer (I wish I had some right now) that does little to combat the vomiting but does induce retroactive amnesia. As I wept with those women who saw me through the most physically intense ordeal of my life, I had the chilling realization I did not know a single one of their names.

They say that times of crisis are the true test of one's character. I really wouldn't know, since my character took a powder that year, leaving in its stead a jewel-bright hardness. I was at my very funniest that year. This was not the Humor of Cure; it had nothing to do with the healing power of laughter. It was more of an airless, relentless kind of quippiness—the orchestra on the *Titanic* playing an upbeat number as they take on water. Every time a complex human emotion threatened to break the surface of my consciousness, out would come some terrible cleverness. Come on, Give Us a Smile!

I was Thanatos' rodeo clown. I still am. And Eros' as well, as it turns out. Years later, in a tender embrace in bed with my first real boyfriend, he said my name. "Oh, David." I stopped, sat up, and responded in my best Ed Wynn, "Yeeeesssssss??????" This kind of behavior more or less killed things between us.

There was a period during the illness when I was at my very sickest, at 115 pounds hovering in and out of consciousness. This month and a half was the one period in my life when I was perhaps not faking it; where I was not deflecting every emotion with repartee. That it would take millions of cancer cells, lining up for their big Esther Williams finale in my lymphatic system, for me to finally shut up is sobering. Or would be were I to think about it.

What remains of your past if you didn't allow yourself to feel it when it happened? If you don't have your experiences in the moment, if you gloss them over with jokes or zoom past them, you end up with curiously dispassionate memories. Procedural and depopulated. It's as if a neutron bomb went off and all you're left with are hospital corridors, where you're scanning the walls for familiar photographs.

Sometimes in the absence of emotion, your only recourse is to surround yourself with objects; assemble the relics about you. Wagner was wrong when he said, "Joy is not in things, it is in us." One can find joy in things, but it is a particular kind of joy—the joy of corroboration. This is why I am once again flying north to try to commune with my little Eskimo Pie children. For the moment, this physical evidence will have to serve as proof that all that has happened was real, because even now I only half believe what I am telling you.

ACKNOWLEDGMENTS

I am grateful to many people, most notably those responsible for many of the pieces in this book: at *This American Life,* Ira Glass, for his extraordinary editorial sensibility, guidance, and friendship; Julie Snyder has been my travel companion, unflagging pal, and Icelandic dance partner; and many thanks as well go to Alix Spiegel, Nancy Updike, Alex Blumberg, Blue Chevigny, Susan Burton, Todd Bachman, and honorable mention to Sarah Vowell, for numberless pep talks and perplexingly unstinting support. At *GQ,* it has been my privilege to work for Jim Nelson, that rarest of creatures, a wonderful writer who is also a gifted and selfless editor. My boys at *Outside*—Mike Grudowski, Adam Horowitz, John Tayman, and Jay Stowe—gave me greater opportunities than I deserved. Alison Humes at *Condé Nast Traveler* showed me enormous patience. At Doubleday, many have made my publishing experience an inordinately happy one: Many thanks to Bill Thomas, who made the first call, and gratitude for the kindness and enthusiasm of Bette Alexander, Ben Bruton, Adrienne Carr, Christopher Litman, Alison Rich, and Linda Steinman. And most especially numberless thanks for the gimlet eye and calming assurance of my editor, Amy Scheibe.

Many friends helped and endured in many ways. Alphabetical thanks and apologies to: Jonathan Adler, Abigail Asher, Laura Barnett, Tracy Behar, Carin Berger, Peter Borland, Janet Byrne, James Carr, Cliff Chase, Chuck Coggins, Randy Cohen, Erin Cramer, Jane Darroch, Emma Davie, Marco DeMartino, Deirdre Dolan, Eamon Dolan, Simon Doonan, Kim Drain, Anne Edelstein, Dave Eggers, John Flansburgh, Susan Friedland, Sheila Gilooly, Robin Goldwasser, Scott Gutterman, Hugh Hamrick, Dan Heymann, Jackie Hoffman, Lutz Holzinger, Jeff Hoover,

Rebecca Johnson, Alexa Junge, Ariel Kaminer, Gillian Katz, Jamie Kay, Trena Keating, Tom Keenan, Chip Kidd, Geoff Kloske, Laura Kurgan, Alisa Lebow, Susan Lehman, Jodi Lennon, Betsy Lerner, Maggie Levine, Hugo Lindgren, Joel Lovell, Cynthia Madansky, Kyoko Makino, Patty Marx, Danielle Mattoon, Jim Millward, Max Moerman, Roy Moskowitz, Mark O'Donnell, Doug Petrie, Stephen Pevner, Greg Pflugfelder, Kate Porterfield, Andy Richter, Scott Riley, Matt Roberts, Phillippe Sands, Chris Santos, Natalia Schiffrin, David Schofield, Deb Schwartz, Mark Scott, Amy Sedaris, Vivian Selbo, Stephen Sherrill, Madhulika Sikka, Corinna Snyder, Ivan Solotaroff, Stoley, David Sternbach, Risaku Suzuki, Jess Taylor, Sarah Thyre, Paul Tough, Bruce Upbin, Rob Weisbach, and Jaime Wolf.

And to my family: Vivian Rakoff, Gina Shochat-Rakoff, Ruth, Tom, Micah, Amit, & Asaf Rakoff-Bellman, Simon Rakoff, Suzy Zucker, and Zoe Zucker Rakoff.

Truthfully, none of this would have ever happened without my agent Irene Skolnick, who waited some twelve years while I got my act together. And to David Sedaris, the man who repeatedly let me know by word and deed that I was still allowed, at the very least, to try.